A RASTAFARIAN
JOURNEY

A RASTAFARIAN JOURNEY

CLYDE EVERTON BRODBER

JANUS PUBLISHING COMPANY
London, England

First published in Great Britain 2001
by Janus Publishing Company Limited,
76 Great Titchfield Street,
London W1P 7AF

www.januspublishing.co.uk

A CIP catalogue record for this book
is available from the British Library

ISBN 1 85756 431 6

Cover design, Creative Line

Printed and bound in Great Britain

1

The Hill

I now remember vaguely, as a little boy growing up in the remote rural village where I lived, climbing the hilly slopes nearby, sitting down on the hillside for brief periods. But I had never had to sit so precariously on any hillside before, I mused to myself, as I perched nervously on one of the makeshift sitting spots dug out of the slopes for the seating of the majority of the Israelites – Rastafarians, qualified to be present on the 'hill'. I can't, indeed, recollect having to sit precariously anywhere, let alone, on a hillside.

I was nervous, very nervous, for various reasons. This was my first experience of the Hill of which I had heard so much in the past months; further, I had always been a fearful, nervous person, especially when overawed, and, perched where I was, this experience seemed just too much for poor, soft-soap, 'fraidy-puss me to ingest calmly.

Always unfortunately subject to anxious thoughts, prone to worrying and negative thinking, I wondered what would be the solution if I needed to urinate. Where would I so do, how would I get to wherever and how would I make it back to my precarious little perch? And failing to make it back, where would I find alternative space from which to address the next hours of meeting on this unaccustomed place, fully covered with these strange people all, like myself, wearing a tam of red, gold and green? The eyes of most glistened, alien-like, in the semi-dark; the smell, totally monopolising the air, was that emanating from what seemed like all-possible varieties of ganja being consumed in vast quantities; out of the reach of the law practically.

A spliff soon found its way to my hand, and within minutes the negative questions vacated my mind, my shoulders relaxed and my hands stopped trembling. Mentally I felt like I had been transported to a different world completely, as I now focused a lot less anxiously on the scenario, a spectacle of which I was now a part, absolutely mind boggling as it all was! I kicked myself and thereby confirmed the reality of it all.

The herb was still fairly new to me at the time; in fact its existence in my life was just months old in my twenty-six years of life. I had not even yet experienced, very significantly, its pleasurable aspects but more saw it as an integral feature of the Rasta faith which I was now embracing. In truth, though, it had helped my shy, introverted person, stilling my inhibitions through many an unaccustomed situation, to the point even that here was I, of all persons, voluntarily seated on this awe-inspiring hill amongst this peculiar gathering. The herb did in fact calm my always nervous hands as did alcohol, but without the accompanying consequential after-effect.

As I settled in my seat, my fright and awe waning substantially, two peanuts reached my hand and I chewed on them for what seemed an eternity as the morsel of food simulated a feast, in my mind. Such was the effect of the herb on my sense of perception.

2

Still, my first experience of herb smoking was terrifying and as such I was now quite scared of ingesting too much, so I hurriedly passed on the spliff, in a manner I immediately realised was too precipitant and smacking more of an intention to get rid of the herb than of sharing it as an offering.

The seasoned 'dreads' sitting behind chuckled at my evident fear of going higher and the manner in which I had passed on the spliff.

I had had involvement which I still maintained administratively with a pop band, in conjunction with my business partner and best friend, Ringo. He had experienced the Hill months before and was indeed instrumental in getting me, plus most of the band's musicians, cross over to this Rasta religion. I was not, therefore, exactly without accustomed company here. Without Ringo especially, I did not know how I would have managed; I did not, even as yet, know how to roll my own spliff, or relate to my new brethren, almost all of them from a different walk of life.

Ringo was unofficially the head of our group. As it turned out, he was from the tribe of Judah, more or less the leadership tribe and the said tribe from which Jesus Christ had sprung and the same that His Imperial Majesty, Emperor Haile Selassie I had indicated he belonged to.

Me? I am of the tribe of Naphtali, so they said; a hind let loose, a speaker of goodly words are some of the characteristics of my tribe. They told me that Naphtali represented the knee on the anatomy, and in the metaphorical body of Christ. He was sort of a linkman in the scheme of things: useful, but certainly not as highly esteemed as Judah.

On the Hill, though, was probably the first I was seeing Ringo overawed, overshone, overrun, I mused as I noticed his usually effervescent self trying too hard to seem to belong in the eyes of our group and others. We were close friends and I knew him well and realised that, in spite of his getting to know the prophet-leader well enough, he, and by extension we, were not yet accepted as genuine, orthodox, full fledged roots brethren. And when my eyes, from my perch, took in the river of red, gold and green headdress of the thousands of brethren and sisters, most dreadlocked, some with face, deportment, mannerisms I would normally have run away from, knowing that underneath our tams were but 'baldheads', I could not help but feel like I was on the fringe, with Ringo slightly less so. And when the dread, dread, dreadlocks behind us borrowed Ringo's stock of herb to fix himself a spliff, Ringo, uncharacteristically, had difficulty in asking back for it, assigning instead coward me to do so!

Ringo, though, had done excellently; he had been instrumental in bringing me to the realisation that I was a chosen of God, and had led me to the house of the chosen, the Twelve Tribes of Israel, along with these other guys.

From my perch, I, concealing my natural fear of heights, followed with my eyes the course of the slopes as they climbed steeply to the pinnacle where a little shack existed. That's one shack, I said to myself, I will never see the inside of, even with the aid of herb. Below me, to the front, was a small levelled area containing makeshift seats, where the women and children sat facing the elders seated similarly, a precipitous slope a few feet away from the back row. To the elders' left some brethren made space for standing where none seemed to exist, a precipitous fall behind them also. Directly in the elders' view, behind the women and children, was a slope, similar to the one on which we were seated, which was filled with brethren. A few brethren found accommodation in trees, and throughout the night there was one shouting intermittently, regularly, insistently, Selassie I, much as a madman would.

A little back down the track, from which I had earlier found my way to my seat, some brothers and a few sisters gathered making purchases from a refreshment shed. As my eyes scanned the hill, my wandering heart and too logical forward-thinking mind wanted to know where space would be found to deal with the monthly increase of membership. Ringo, in a sternish voice, chided me saying, 'Jah will provide', as yet another spliff reached me. In spite of my wish not to climb any higher mentally, refusal being impossible I employed faith and took a few pulls before passing it on. The natural noises of the night now became as clear as if they originated in my ear. More relaxed physically, I looked at the moon, the stars, the skies and it seemed as if I was seeing creation for the first time as these creations of my Father seemed to wink back at me deliberately. My vision landed again on the great multitude here gathered and I was dumbstruck as hundreds, all colour faces, all sorts and appearances, offered me a sight never seen or closely simulated before in my entire life. I felt both fear and comfort: comfort in belonging to such a large awe-inspiring brotherhood, comfort in being a part of a movement which, to my mind, was similar to that of Jesus the Christ when he trod earth. My fear was of the trials and tribulations certainly ahead, from the scribes and Pharisees, the high priests and Babylon as a whole, its systems set up to persecute and eradicate us, the people of God.

And when my herb-tinted eyes made four with those of my various brethren, theirs glistened in the dark of the night like diamonds. This whole new unaccustomed scenario was simply mind-boggling to me so far.

I had been a successful salesman and budding businessman and as such possessed a flashy wardrobe consistent with that status, but now had painstakingly searched out my shabbiest outfit not to appear inconsistent with the clothing of the brethren as I anticipated it to be on the Hill. I had tried my best, how recently, to appear as 'roots' as I could in light of the fact that my brethren, most of them, were predominantly ghetto poor.

Still, the drive to the foot of the Hill, my first, was awe-inspiring to me, being unfortunately nervously apt to invoke anxiety tremors by my proclivity to negative anticipation. And, in truth, I was uncertain of the reception I would receive from the brethren, especially in view of the fact that I was an upwardly mobile 'uptowner' seeking a piece of the 'roots-man's' proud heritage. And as always I was absolutely terrified of making glaring errors that might reap ridicule and embarrassment, two of my most dreaded enemies.

Ringo, my friend, as usual had made things easier for me by driving in front. The other boys from the band, making their inaugural trip to the Hill like myself, travelled some with him, some with me. These made the trip less traumatic for me. Along the way strewn with red, gold and green capped persons, we filled our cars beyond legal limit with other brothers and sisters.

At the foot of the Hill it was a sight to behold. Not one many people could imagine. There were 'dreadlocks' of every size, shape, mannerism, look, plus 'baldheaded' dreads milling around at the tiny entrance, intermingling. Rastafarians of head and or heart of the Twelve Tribes of Israel, from every part of the country, and visiting from abroad, were greeting one another enthusiastically. I even recognised and spoke with some persons of earlier acquaintance whom I had always admired but had not seen for a long time. Here they were, having some time before escaped the system, the society, the existing status quo, into the house of the chosen – the Twelve Tribes of Israel Rastafarian movement. I could see Ringo enthusiastically hailing many of the brethren. Not all appeared to me to be reciprocating his warm greeting.

I could not prevent my mind staying on those I had just re-met, especially those from school days. Their spirit, their personality, their character I had always liked and admired: here they were in the 'house', which I was now becoming a part of. It then seemed to me as if we were in fact the chosen handpicked by the Almighty long ago. This realisation helped to lessen somewhat the tremoring in my body and mind at the prospect of this, my initial visit to the Hill.

We started the ascent. How I hate climbing hills, especially on narrow trails, slipping and sliding with unsure feet and nervous self-conscious demeanour, whilst others, including women, are trekking merrily on, problem free, unintentionally making me out to be a 'sap'. How the hell will I make it down this perilous trail after meeting-late tonight/tomorrow morning without embarrassing myself? Prayer and faith, I answered myself.

The free-flow progress uphill ceased as the order floated down, 'single file' and Ringo informed us 'newies' to get out our 'dues books', the passport beyond this point. No one without his 'banner' the red, gold and green headdress passed this point either.

Eventually I reached the top of the line and, dues book inspected, I moved on up, feeling most emphatically as if I had literally moved into the House of Israel leaving 'Babylon' and all it stood for behind. My brethren Ringo led us on to the available perches on one of which I am now settling, with the aid of the herb trying to make myself as comfortable as possible given the conditions geographical and personal.

I surveyed all around me with my mouth open in awe, consternation, shock and all else related to witnessing and being part of a scene which felt like, and seemed like, Moses/Joshua and the Israelites seated for a meeting, or Jesus Christ and his followers doing likewise. This simply and truthfully is how it seemed and felt to me, probably because I had recently been reading so much Bible; probably because my mentor Ringo had led me to this thinking and certainly as a result of the herb high, which made me think on a different plane, a higher plane. But it most definitely appeared so to me.

The scene was just too much from so many perspectives.

Here I was, nervous me, of all persons, looking with the eyes of a man considered 'uptown', sitting perched from where, with a wrong move, I could easily fall, sliding embarrassingly down amongst the sisters and children, disrupting on this my first visit this righteous government, to be, of God.

Try sitting where you can't move, space very limited and you unable to retrace your steps to your seat if you should manage to venture away from it, seeing simultaneously a couple thousand 'dreads', some dread, dread, dread, all and sundry in bright red, gold and green 'banners', you not as yet even starting to think through the process of 'locksing', and all associated with such a societally defiantly bold move. And when my eyes set on the twelve male elders bedecked in their various robes bearing the colours of the tribe each represented, and Sister Dinah in her special multi-coloured dress, my mouth opened even wider.

The Hill

I had visited, over the past months, the non-exclusive meetings of the organisation held to introduce the 'organ' to all and sundry but this exclusive gathering of members made those meetings, and all else I had been exposed to in life, pale by comparison; and the meeting had not even started as yet.

As yet another spliff reached me I took a pull, pondering on some of the things I had learned concerning the beliefs of the organ. With fixity of focus I zeroed in on the thought of dry bones come to life as described in Ezekiel 37. We the chosen, the Twelve Tribes of Israel, were those rejected dry bones, now brought back to life. The spirits within us, that now lived, were those of the original Israelites some of whom walked with Christ in that dispensation. The prophet, our prophet, resting in the shack at the top of the Hill, had been sent by God to gather the flock by awakening the spirits within us to our enviable identity of chosen by God Almighty.

To me, though still awed by it all, this was more than I had bargained for from life – to be a chosen of the Creator. And when I focused, now quite high on the herb, on the elders once again, it seemed almost unmistakably this time that these bodies housed the spirits of the disciples of Christ, just as Ringo had expressed. I knew also from what I had seen up to now and how I now felt, that I was almost certain that I was indeed present in the House of God.

The serious Bible readings, the non-exclusive meetings before, the reasonings with the prophet and some brethren, the strange inexplicable occurrences and experiences within mind and body in recent times, the 'miracles', had been conversion enough; but now this ambience, this feeling, this whole situation was the clincher. All I now needed prior to diving in fully, irrespective of consequences, was to experience this entire meeting.

9

The command, 'One voice', from the Levite elder caused, within seconds, a silence that would have allowed you to hear a pin drop on the dirt, except for some faint sounds coming from the refreshment area; but the repeated command addressed to that area evoked absolute silence, as you could sense, even touch almost, the near tangible anticipation.

On the issue of the command 'One voice' I searched out, with my eyes, and found the international reggae king, who I had seen arrive earlier. The order had made him, just like innocuous me, as quiet as a lamb. An order like that was an order to one and all, great and small. This impressed me significantly.

With the Levite elder on his feet, his Bible open in his hand, the meeting was about to begin in earnest, all spliffs, pipes were to be extinguished, for the time being.

Having allowed some seconds for the required atmosphere of respectful serenity, Levi started the creed. The entire membership joined in 'for the preachers of the Cross is to them that perish ... foolishness but to us who are saved it's the power of God ...' His Bible reading, which followed, was taken from the Book of Ezekiel, chapter 37. Other tribe elders then shared Bible readings before some from the general membership were allowed to read theirs, with the understanding that members who had not completed the Bible, reading a chapter a day progressively, were not allowed to read a full chapter.

Each elder of the first executive, including Sister Dinah, then addressed the membership after which some from the general membership were allowed to do likewise.

The communications which followed, from brethren all over the world, but especially those from Ethiopia, touched me exceedingly. They all reminded me so much of the Epistles to and from the likes of St Paul when the message of

10

The Hill

Christianity had just been understood and was being dis-
seminated.

New members were now formally introduced as the name
of each was called to the cheers of the membership. As our
names were called the lightning flashed and the thunder
rolled and the membership accepted this as a seal of approval
from our God the Creator. To me it appeared as if the Creator,
the God of the Heavens and the Earth, was indeed listening in
on these His children.

After the public financial accounting session, in which all
participated, was concluded under the direction of the Asherite
elder, the floor was open for matters pertaining to activities
within the house: notices plus any other relevant matters.
There were football matters, cricket matters, dancing club,
music matters and a myriad of miscellaneous matters cover-
ing a very wide cross-section impacting on individual members of the organ as a whole. There were matters related to
inner and outer membership disputes also.

All eyes watched his descent from the shack at the pinnacle.
He floated down the treacherous hill with absolute confidence and speed, as if fear was a dismissed consideration
from his being. Resplendent in his red robe, he sailed on
down with a purposeful and stern look on his face, his eyes
blazing and glistening in a superhuman manner. I wondered
if this was the same person I had met and conversed with a
few times before.

Herb smoking had restarted after the Scripture readings
and now you could see many a spliff, many a pipe being
lighted up to reach the ideal frame of mind to tune in to, to
take in every word that came from the mouth of the prophet,
one like Moses returned to us.

There was no doubt this was the moment everyone was

waiting for. Brethren had travelled from all parts of the island, including the uttermost parts; some were visiting from overseas, some, mostly young ones, had left home against the wishes of parents/guardians. Some would lose their jobs tomorrow having been found out to be members of the Rasta movement. All and sundry, members of the House of Israel, had come to hear the current prophet of the Twelve Tribes of Israel. Me, I just sat there stunned, looking in total admiration, bewilderment and respect at this person who had the most direct line to the Creator, this person to whom it was given to rise up the Twelve Tribes of Israel, this person who had caused me to know that I, nervous me, was a chosen one, and needed worry no more for the God of Heaven, the God of Creation, now knew me by name, and eternal life was mine indeed if I but continued to do that which I knew was right.

This man, the likeness of Moses, had brought to an end the religious search I had embarked on. I had found the truth.

His manner of speaking was far from grammatically correct but if you listened closely enough to understand, he made great sense, was logical and demonstrated more knowledge, wisdom and understanding than I had ever been exposed to.

He had a stern look, usually, but that often and easily melted, exposing a kind, compassionate, thoughtful spirit with a passion for justice and equality. The membership seemed to love and 'worship' him.

Even newcomer me seemed to be totally enraptured as I picked up every word that fell from the prophet's mouth; and when he said, 'We have got to beat down Babylon', I was prepared to throw the first stone. When he said, 'There are spies amongst us; one day we may have to hang one of them from one of these trees', I saw myself as part of the lynching mob.

He evoked from us all mutual love, compassion and brotherhood but also anger and rebellious thoughts against the existing unjust system. I felt like a revolutionary wishing to 'bomb a church now I knew that the preacher was lying'.

The prophet carried us through his purpose here on earth, in this dispensation; how he was called to duty, and the recognition of himself and his role. He gave us a history of his life and of this organisation of which he was the founder.

He exhorted the brethren to do right; he implored us to love one another; he reinforced the fact that we were the hand-picked chosen ones, who were called to duty and should proceed on our work with dedication and commitment, knowing that we had the backing of the Almighty God and good would overcome evil.

Of Jesus Christ he said, and I listened even more intently, 'We have no dispute that He is the Son of God who went through death as a mortal to set us free from sins and to open up for us life eternal. As Emmanuel He was indeed God with us. Where we differ with the others is that we know, with absolute certainty, that He has, in these days, returned to earth in the person of His Imperial Majesty Emperor Haile Selassie I.' The Hill erupted in thunderous applause, and those who throughout the meeting kept chanting 'Selassie I' upped the mania to the point that, as the prophet broke to allow the outpouring, the whole hill, including me, rang out with the chant 'Selassie I', and I was sure the whole city must have heard, and must have shaken with fear.

Of all the Rasta matters to date, this was the principal area, Selassie I as God, which I was having difficulty digesting. Although it had been explained to me before, tonight was the first time I felt convinced. Jesus Christ I had always loved and could still love. In time, I would accept Him in His new personality: that as His Imperial Majesty, Emperor Haile Selassie I.

It was now into the wee hours of the morning, and I couldn't help but think of my wife at home She would surely be worried for me, but my developing faith told me that I was about my Father's business, so she would be just fine.

My mind stayed on her somewhat, nonetheless. I had, less than a year ago, married this wonderful, beautiful gem of a young woman whom I loved dearly. Could she accept this new me, who had previously tried to escape this call but couldn't? If I could only convince her of this truth I had discovered, everything would be just fine. How could she, from her background, accept that this unimpressive looking ghetto man with missing teeth was indeed the true prophet of God, in this time? Faith, I said to myself, faith in God, as I refocused on the prophet of God.

Some brethren were now being brought up before the prophet as his austere look reappeared. Some were chided strongly and warned, some were suspended from the Hill and I thought of the disgrace associated with being cut off from the House of Israel, and there and then made my resolution to behave in a manner exemplary at all times, lest I too find myself excommunicated.

Many brethren, too, were congratulated and commended for various good deeds, and as their faces beamed with pride, I made my resolution: to find myself, one day, in that category.

After the prophet had continued and finished, Levi rose to duty again in leading the meeting in the singing of the hymn, this time 'Blest be the tie that binds...'

Thereafter, the meeting coming to a close, he advised us all to be careful on our way to our various destinations. 'Those who live in volatile areas, where possible, should stay on the Hill until sunrise. Try not to travel alone but in groups, and remember don't travel with the herb, except in your head. Some will nonetheless get locked up but each one must help the other, all for one and one for all in a combat against the enemy. Those who drive must leave with their vehicles full, giving preference to the children and the sisters.'

We all then faced the north as we sang the Ethiopian anthem with our hands on our hearts.

I was thrilled, converted, committed, pleased to have been selected, a chosen in the revised House of Israel, God's own people.

Many lingered on the Hill; I, Naphtali, waited around a bit as Ringo Judah, characteristically, mingled amongst the brethren. 'What a meeting ... the "Hill" was so sweet ... guidance and protection my brethren', were some of the comments amongst brethren and sisters.

It was after I made it to the foot of the Hill that I remembered my fear of the journey down, so I duly gave thanks to Jah, the ever faithful God, ever faithful, ever living, ever sure.

All around me was a sea of red, gold and green. Some brethren were walking, some running, some on bicycles, some on motorcycles, a few motor vehicles. This I knew would be the pattern throughout the day as the membership wended their way home to all parts of the island.

After dropping off various people at various points, I made it safely home as the day began to break into light. I gave thanks again for not having been stopped by the police as I entered my middle-class home. I could see my wife was worried, but knowing I had to catch a quick rest prior to getting ready for work, she questioned me not. As I was dozing off, I told her I had found truth indeed, and wished to share it with her.

Travelling to work, I did so with a completely different mental attitude than formerly. My head was still stuck in the meeting on the Hill.

From my upstairs office, I could see, not far off, on a sidewalk, the brother who sold mats and hammocks. He had apparently come straight from the meeting and was unpacking his bags to display his wares as he had been doing, at this spot, even before I started my religious search. As I reminisced, I could hardly keep my mind on my job throughout that day. Christ had been put in perspective, likewise His Majesty, the Bible, Israel. I now understood why I, despite reasonable financial success, found it so difficult to be a part of Babylon, its systems, its politics, its government, its corruption.

The prophecies of the Bible, even Revelation, took on more meaning and relevance to me, and eternal life became something real, meaningful, graspable.

The creation, the world, money, sex now all had a simple story which made sense to me.

The spirit within man, brotherly love, mankind, Ethiopia, Africa were additional subject areas that were finding new meaning and passionate interest within my headspace and by extension, my life.

Importantly, some people were being terribly unjust to some and these chosen people were being awfully abused and downtrodden and persecuted because, like in the days of Christ, they wanted the will of God done, not the will of the devil-controlled world.

I had done some serious Bible reading over the last months of search and realised that what I had been taught before by spiritual leaders could almost be classified as foolishness relative to the truth I was now seeing for myself in the pages of the Scriptures. And in fact, as I read through the prophets, this innocuous looking man reminded me more of those I had read of than any other person I had met in my entire life. And quite frankly, hearing him, seeing him in action last night, had clinched it. He was indeed a prophet.

I wasn't exactly totally okay with his Majesty – Selassie I – evidentially, but last night did feel as if the gathering had a direct line to God and at the shouts of worship to Selassie I the thunder did seem to roar and the lightning flash in response. And of a truth I have never seen anywhere a God worshipped with so much gusto, passionate love and absolute reverence. Only a religious vehicle like this could satisfy my passion and deep commitment, I knew; only an organisation like this could soothe and satisfy my soul; in fact this is what I had been searching for, in terms of substance.

In spite of my past sins, inclusive of countless cases of fornication, I had sought escape from sin and forgiveness and had now been offered a place in the House of God, an opportunity at eternal life as a child of the tribe of Naphtali.

I, this moment, that day, vowed to take up the mantle and join this fight for truth and right, irrespective of the consequences.

I would soon have to resign this job, lucrative as it was, I said to myself, as I tried strenuously to refocus on my sales job; the two were simply incompatible.

I had met with tremendous success in my job as a real estate salesman, and had in fact, last year, topped the field in spite of my introverted self and other personal limitations. I had married well, one I loved and admired, I had material possessions belying my reasonably humble material start and my age of twenty-six. However, I had been unfulfilled, with numerous important questions unanswered. The answers I had received from the recognised existing religious-spiritual quarters were simply not convincing enough, so I had started searching for myself, reading all the religious matter I could get my hands on, eventually ending up right back in the Holy Bible which I had before discarded, along with church-going, as soon as such decisions were mine to make solely.

Ringo had been bitten by the 'search bug' before and, characteristically, jumped ahead of me in his search for the truth. His search had led him to the Holy Bible which had proven to him that the Twelve Tribes of Israel was the righteous vehicle of God, and, by extension, the Rastafarian way of life was the right way.

Ringo was courageous, adventurous and personable and was not afraid to go 'underground', if necessary, to get close to and reason with the brethren. In fact for the past year, almost, he had pulled away from the working scene to study life and find truth. When he found the truth he came to share it with me and started dragging me along to meet the brethren and the prophet.

In time he 'stepped up' to be numbered amongst the chosen whilst I resisted in spite of the numerous 'general' meetings he took me to and the numerous brethren he had reason with me. One, a Joseph brethren, dressed in his rags, reminded me of Jesus Christ. You could see the abundance of humility and compassion flowing from him.

Mingling with the brethren I found myself, more and more, having to participate in herb smoking.

For months, I tagged along on the outskirts of the movement, seeing and accepting that this doctrine was, for most parts, consistent with what I now knew of the Bible and certainly sounded much more authentically religious than anything else I knew of. In fact this doctrine sounded very much like the truth, but the big step was just too much for my courage.

I lost myself in bible study even more, often communally with Ringo and other brethren. Secretly I hoped to find flaws in their interpretation and in time to discover the truth as being related to a more acceptable route. That was not to be, and I began meeting with Ringo and the others more regularly. I still had fear of the inevitable herb smoking at these meetings, but saw it as anti-social, and cowardly in appearance, not to partake of the passing spliffs. I did find out though that with the herb my mental vision focused more penetratingly, unearthing profound seeming truths about life. I started at the time also undergoing some inexplicable experiences which to my mind fell in the ranks of supernatural. I would, for example, awaken at nights and see the face of His Majesty Emperor Haile Selassie I unmistakably glowing on the wall, as if from an invisible projector. I can also remember experiencing a feeling of levitation as my spirit left my body nightly, travelling the earth. Of course these are things that had never happened to me before, just like how I would but wish for something and it just happened to reach me in short time without apparent effort on my part.

I noticed also that the herb had the capacity to release me from my inhibitions which I daily had tried so hard to conceal and, in the process, it made me courageous enough to do things I would not have attempted before.

Ringo, too, seemed so much wiser since his search, and particularly now that he had found truth, 'stepped up' and smoked the herb regularly. He would tell me how the brethren I had met and reasoned with would, on the Hill, always enquire if I hadn't yet escaped Babylon and 'come over' into life.

He had almost given up on me. The one meeting he was absent from happened, ironically, to be the one at which I found the courage to 'step up'. I did so, though with great trepidation and fear, not thinking the move reversible. It was as if a great burden had eventually been released from my shoulders, and was I welcomed joyously into God's House!

To get my dues book involved taking two passport pictures to the centre at which dues were paid at twenty cents per week.

My dues book in hand, I had qualified for the Hill, and I received the commissioned banner from the Zebulite sister.

2

Concerning my Conversion

In the mid 1970s, like most times during my life, Rasta, socio-economically, occupied the lowest rung on the ladder. It was a cult predominantly of the poor, of the black, of those poor blacks considered mad, mad enough to spurn material progress, speak a funny tongue and be foolish enough to consider and worship Haile Selassie, the Ethiopian African King, as God. If one was to choose the scum of the society, over the years, ever since the inception of the movement then Rasta would have been considered it in the perception of most people. In the mid 1970s though, a few light-skinned, even white-skinned persons, blacks also from middle-class stations and a few from the upper echelons, had dived down into the Rasta cult, the Twelve Tribes of Israel branch especially.

Next to or equal to death was the pain of some parents to the revelation that a son or daughter had decided to become a Rastafarian.

Rasta was formerly really a religious cult with attractiveness almost exclusively to a few of the very poor. The elite scorned it, the middle classes, the majority of the poor even,

21

scorned Rasta as if they were, in fact, the lowest rung of the ladder of human existence.

The Rastaman had, in previous years, developed a notorious reputation in many regards. He was reputed, for example, in the earlier days, to be the 'blackheart man', the man who stole away little children to cut out for evil purposes their hearts; unjustified claims like those arose because the Rastaman was so very different from the rest of society, and so very little was actually known of what he stood for. Moreover, what little was known was so different and strange to the ears of the majority, that fear and mystique and hate and scorn resulted from the distorted information that reached the citizenry, certainly in the early days of the cult.

His manner of existence was indeed peculiar. He lived in the distant hills far away from the normal materialistic culture, doing a little farming to feed himself and dependents. The ganja herb was significant to his way of life and he smoked it almost constantly, usually from a chillum pipe. His hair was uncombed so that it grew into long thick, uncared for, awe-inspiring locks, like his beard. His clothing was not conventional by any stretch of the imagination, and all told he appeared like a mad, awe-inspiring being from the distant mountains, much like a wild animal. On top of all this, he worshipped a living man as God to the absolute dismay of Christian and other societies.

In the 1970s when I was getting involved, Rastas were no longer exclusive to the hills, and society as a whole knew more, understood more and did not exactly any more run from the blackheart man, though they still scorned him. There were, of course, some branches that still maintained that great distance from society but not the Twelve Tribes of Israel, which had reached out with their message across the socio-economic borders, to a small extent, touching even the lives of Ringo and myself and others like us.

Twelve Tribes came with a doctrine which they were willing and able to explain, one that was more than palatable and desirable to some of us. They promised a real close existence with God; to the extent that a believer felt special, especial to the Almighty God, as if chosen by Him to be a child and servant of His. And, in fact, Jesus Christ was recognised as the Son of God but now revealed, in His kingly character, in the person of His Imperial Majesty, Emperor Haile Selassie I, King of Kings and Lord of Lords. Before and during my deep involvement with the organisation, quite a few people from the various levels of the middle class, dropouts some, took the plunge down into this Rasta movement, claiming their right as being of the chosen, espousing passionately the doctrine of truth and right. To our loved ones though, we had taken a plunge into the bottomless pit, from which they knew not whether we would resurface, ever.

In the view of my peers, my wife included, there was no more surprising a turn I could have taken. Certainly to my father, stepmother, brothers and sisters, and in-laws, I had lost my mind and my way totally, inexplicably.

My joining this Rasta movement was, to everyone, almost like walking in the opposite direction of progress, to say the least. Indeed a Rastaman's life was still, to the system as a whole, worth nothing much, expendable except to the extent that the mystery surrounding him and his commitment to peace and love, purity and the scriptures created a doubt in the minds of the authorities. Restraining also to the authorities was the fact that quite a few now inside the movement were sons, daughters, and relatives of theirs.

* * *

Oh how my friends and I had laughed at this character who hung out with us, called Double X, the first Rasta-minded person to get that close to me. I was about twenty years old at the time and was finding X an absolute idiot as he filled our heads with this Rasta foolishness claiming Selassie to be God Almighty. His stories concerning the miraculous exploits of the Ethiopian Emperor evoked more ridicule as he told us, among other things, how his God had kicked away a would-be assassin's bullets without even damaging his shoes.

In time, however, Double X conceded victory to us and started chasing money and women with the same unholy gusto and passion we did then.

A few years later, the instrument-lifter within the pop band was a Rasta-minded ghetto man. This was the second time Rasta foolishness was invading my space and did this fellow pelt our ears with the claims to divinity of Ras Tafari, Selassie! I was particularly annoyed when at the solution of any problem he ascribed verbally and loudly thanks and praises to Jah Rastafari, Selassie I.

I was at the time, whilst co-managing the band to a national popularity, blazing a trail as a real estate salesman, with no one probably, besides Ringo, knowing the real me: a shy, introverted guy with a massive inferiority chip on his shoulder.

Success, however, was slowly bringing confidence and belief in myself.

I succeeded because I approached everything I did with a consuming passion that pulled from me 100 per cent at least. Not being mentally that quick on my feet, I would work through the night rehearsing, to perfection, my tomorrow's sales presentations. Also, I spent quantity and quality time planning and organising my work. I was enthusiastic and industrious and reaped rewards commensurately.

Not being, to any stretch of the imagination, outstandingly physically attractive, I employed similar tactics in the field of womanising and managed to snare, sexually, too many women for my burdensome conscience, founded on strict Christian early upbringing, to accept unconcerned.

I had acquired some valuable real estate holdings including my upper-middle income house. I had a promising career in my chosen profession, equity interest and management control in the successful pop band; I had enough to afford and opportunity to enjoy great revelry, and my financial commitments were up to date. I was living a comfortable lifestyle, had numerous friends, a 'with it' wardrobe, supportive family and in-laws who all seemed to love me.

Why the hell would I, given this enviable status and lifestyle, become a Rasta, of all things?

This same question I have asked myself for probably the billionth time, not prepared to accept the theory that I was an absolute fool. I know there was more to it, much more.

Being involved with the band and exposed daily to the music of the day, I couldn't but hear and feel the cry of the downpressed for a better country, a better world, free from the existing oppressive system, inclusive of the Church. The cry was for freedom, justice and equality. Those were the days of rebel music; and if there was one thing I abhorred with consummate passion, it was injustice of any kind, at any level.

It was also a time of 'search'; and, to me, if a young man was not searching for his roots, the meaning of life, the truth, a better way for mankind, then he was 'dealing with nothing'.

An inspection of the existing religious institutions within the system confirmed to me, at the time, that what I was seeking for did not lie in that arena. In fact, the concealed rebel in me was emerging with introverted pent up venom now that I realised that even the Church was just a façade: concealing, too, the wrongs of an unjust system.

Awakened to the reality that all was not as it appeared to be, I started looking at other aspects of the existing system and found them all wanting and seeming like a grand cover up of all forms of wickedness.

Now that, for example, I was for the first time in my life speaking 'one and one' with genuine ghetto brethren, I got firsthand knowledge of some truths. When, heretofore some feebly heard cries escaped from the ghettos that youths were being forced to take guns to fight political wars against the rival parties, our eminent leaders on both sides had denied these as lies, rubbish, and, of course, we uptown had believed them. Now I knew, undoubtedly, that it was our eminent leaders who were lying and as a result the rebel in me boiled inwardly.

I had also believed the police hierarchy when they had denied accusations of abuse, brutality and general prejudice against the poor. These accusations I now learnt were absolutely true, and the abuses stark, glaring, constant, unabated and well concealed.

I was finding out that the system was based on, perpetuated, and concealed what seemed disgraceful wickedness and injustices; and of all things I was a part of this same unconscionable system. If someone had awakened my naïve mind to this situation before I would not then have felt so deceived, shocked, and rebellious.

I didn't know that my thirst and enthusiasm for money, sex

and power could fade. But all of a sudden they did. Those desires, now, all seemed inadequate for my needs as the spirit within me emerged, desirous of greater fulfilment with truth, real truth, right, equality and justice.

I began reading all I could get my hands on of a religious nature – Moslem, Hindu, Black Muslim, Hare Krishna even – but none of these satisfied the needs of my spirit, in my search for God and truth.

One of the questions befuddling my naïvely-inclined mind was why did some of us, who had not necessarily lived exemplary lives, have so much, including status and a home away from the oppression, whilst some, probably better persons, were subjected to such inhumane existence? I had many other unanswered questions but this one, somehow, kept haunting me most.

All of a sudden everything, everything now seemed all so superficial, looking at life as I now did through brand new eyes and a totally different mindset, motivation and spirituality.

Death, a possibility I hadn't much considered, except at funerals, was now a reality that I realised could happen any time, certainly in time, and as such was a consideration that should be factored into and influence the quality of one's lifestyle here on earth. Suppose death caught me now, I reasoned, what would be my lot in the hereafter, given so many sins, mostly sexual, on my record? As a result I submerged myself in and quickened my pace toward the search to find God, the truth, my purpose in life, and a means of atonement for past sins.

Ringo, in the meantime, had eventually found what he was sure was the absolute truth and sought to convince me accordingly. His Rasta story wasn't exactly what I had hoped for, but I listened and analysed and eventually delved into the Scriptures of the Holy Bible, passionately, hoping somewhat that Ringo was wrong. I had to admit, though, that the Bible was predominantly about the Twelve Tribes of Israel. Also, characters like Moses, Samson, John the Baptist and many others, Jesus the Christ even, came across to me as 'dreadlocks'.

The mature secretary at the office, seeing the intensity of my search and my passionate commitment to find, and seeing me inclining to Ringo's Rasta arguments, introduced me to positive imaging as an alternative and gave me a book on the subject. This option was simply not enough for my current needs, especially since my over-enthusiastic study of the Bible was now unearthing for me so many truths, truths which made all other sources of knowledge pale, very pale by comparison.

When I set out, I never, in my wildest dreams, expected that my search would end in a Rasta or like-kind belief. When it did, I tried to escape, but found this futile. The evidence was overpowering; the Bible, the live prophet, Ringo, the deception of that existing as the system, the reggae music, emanating almost exclusively from the ghetto, the brethren, all pointed me to the Twelve Tribes of Israel as the vehicle of truth and right. And when, around the time I thought of escaping, inexplicable supernatural occurrences started touching me, I knew the search had really ended whether I wanted to accept the end result or not.

Eventually I 'stepped up', consoling myself at first with my new-found status as a chosen. I accepted my new status, dived in with my full passion and commitment, resigning my job in the process, prepared to take on the enemy, Babylon.

Concerning my Conversion

I was born in Jamaica, in a small remote rural district, in the parish of St Mary, peopled totally by poor humble folks. Fortunately, my mother was a respected teacher and my father one of the more successful farmers, so my upbringing was less poverty stricken than most of my friends within the community.

Education was something I was exposed to very early. My two sisters, the first children of the union, had established very good academic records. My older brother was not brilliant but good enough. My younger brother was not born until I was four.

Mama was also the organist for our little Anglican church, whilst Papa was a lay preacher. Consequently we all grew up in the Church, knowing the importance of adherence to the Christian principles of right and wrong. Nonetheless, I committed many wrongs, like lying to Papa to avoid a beating, like taking food without permission and lying about having so done, like having sex, time and time again, with the village girls of similar age, before I was nine. God was watching and certainly did punish, via Papa, and more often Mama, when any of such infractions came to light.

During this phase, I never heard much mention of Rasta, but I heard of the 'blackheart man' and knew that if unprotected, I should flee from anyone bearing semblance to what we perceived such a one to be.

I sought the company of my friends when going places, running errands, for indeed I was given to great fear, yet though I was a very private person, confiding in none regarding my deep-seated phobia in relation to being laughed at, embarrassed, ridiculed by anybody.

In those early days I loved to experiment and did so,

privately. At church I had heard that faith could move mountains and tried to do a lesser thing like opening the locked kitchen door solely with faith. I was unsuccessful, and thereafter dubious about that spiritual claim.

I was one hell of a 'dreamer' and always saw myself starring in all sorts of roles. And when I consumed, passionately, the numerous story books I read, I found myself and the star character merging into one until I finished that book, started another and became one with this new star character. When I was not eating, sleeping, reading or playing cricket I was daydreaming, accomplishing, in my dreams, marvellous things single handedly.

Shortly before my tenth birthday, I moved to Kingston to board with relatives in order to start high school.

This phase of my life was not a good one, certainly as far as personal development was concerned. I lost my way academically, I lost, further, my confidence in self and resultantly gave birth to a massive inferiority complex. Going to church, an earlier developed habit, became a chore I had to be coerced into fulfilling, and as a result I lost my way further in terms of spiritual development.

Where I boarded, I was subjected to quite inhumane treatment of a destructive nature, which, apart from damaging my youthful psyche, my confidence and self-esteem et cetera, created in me a nervousness which, at great pains, and fearing ridicule, I tried to conceal.

Though usually in the company of friends and interacting verbally, my deep thoughts and hurt I shared with no one, as I became deep inside a more private person, harbouring deep down massive doses of resentment, bitterness, anger, rage and hate. And to add insult to injury, I simply could not find the courage to approach any of the beautiful girls my soul so desired, and had to be content to romance them in my dreams and daydreams.

To most, high schooling meant important foundational development en route to a meaningful, fulfilling, successful future. I had simply lost my way in almost every regard and, even at the sport of cricket in which I had some sort of talent, I performed way below potential, not being able to rise above my anxiety, nervousness and lack of confidence.

My school's playing field was located near some hills in which lived some Rastas, the children of whom would venture down to the field, raggedly attired, their uncombed hair falling in knotty, untidy dreadlocks. They scared the daylight out of me as I wondered how any human being could exist in this manner, and whether they were human at all!

My few exam passes qualified me for entry to business college, and I managed to pick up the last available space to the relevant facility.

In the two years of college, I managed improvement academically and socially, but the chip, already indented on my shoulder, was too deep for repair. On graduation, I therefore at eighteen years of age, entered the working world a nervous man with a massive inferiority complex and myriad other psychological problems, in addition to an absence of purpose, direction and respectable values.

Mama had died four years earlier and Papa had remarried; my older sister had married and lived in foreign lands. My elder brother had just, one year before me, graduated from college and was attending to his own problems. My other sister had recently returned from studies abroad, and I went to live with her.

Had I received more parental or mature-person guidance, would life have been better? Certainly, if I had boarded where

31

more loving care existed, I would not have been entering the working world so bereft of positive character, and certainly not with so much repressed hurt and anger filling my soul.

Early working life, as a clerk in the office of a utility company, was, at first, not boring, simply because working life was novel to me. Soon, however, I felt as if I was marking time whilst watching paint dry.

I enjoyed a good romantic relationship with a sister of a co-worker. This apart, not much of real interest was happening in my life.

It was in this period of my life that I encountered Double X, espousing, annoyingly, his Rasta doctrine.

After departing this job, I stumbled into an opportunity to sell real estate, and grabbed it. Being introverted, shy and adversely affected psychologically, in many regards I was not well qualified to sell real estate, or anything else. Additionally, which prospective purchaser or seller would take me, at the tender age of twenty, seriously enough? My performance, initially, reflected this. In time, I brought into play my commitment and passion, very hard work, planning, organisation, and general likeableness, and positive rewards resulted.

I started out using my brother's car, when he was at work, but soon acquired my own and before I resigned, on committing myself to the Rasta movement, approximately six years later, I had purchased seven different motor cars each better than the previous, among other assets.

In time I realised that, in spite of the negatives in my character, I was good at real estate sales. Almost every prospect I took out I was able to convert to a sale, and where they thought they could not afford the purchase I devised ingenuous ways how they could. As time went on, and success mushroomed into more success my confidence increased, though I still had to devise ways of concealing the constant nervousness which was potentially embarrassing.

I was now making money, good money, and I was recognised by my peers as being successful. For the first time in life I was developing a belief in myself. And was I having fun! Fun to me then was defined as money, recognition and, of course, sex. Additionally, Ringo and myself were managing the pop band to popularity.

It was during this band involvement that I encountered the equipment lifter who showered my ears irritatingly with his Rasta garbage.

At a band rehearsal, I had uncharacteristically taken a few pulls from the spliff of Ringo who, by this time, was well en route in his search for truth and was much into the herb. I had not then enjoyed the experience of the high but did note how very rhythmically I responded to the music, and also how calm my usually nervous hands were. Previously, I had used alcohol to calm my hands but I hated the later reaction. The herb left me with no such nausea but I did not like aspects of the experience, and vowed not to use this thing again.

The year before my conversion I had broken, so they said, real estate sales records. Soon after, this meant nothing to me as I started my search for the real truth and withdrew my enthusiasm, commitment and hard work, to place them elsewhere.

3

Initial Impact

My dear wife must have felt as if she was hit by a ton of bricks
when I dumped this strange Rasta 'shit' on her with such
conviction.

I had by then withdrawn my vow not to use the herb and
was now smoking it not too infrequently. She must have been
very concerned over my new-found smoking habit, and over
my withdrawal from economic pursuit and desire for upward
mobility. I, of all persons, always seeking to make a sale, was
now not interested in any aspect of serious business activity,
being preoccupied only with reading the Bible, reasoning
with Rasta brethren and wasting gas going to and fro, sup-
posedly working this 'farm', without any knowledge or
experience in the field.

Concerned she must have been over my wearing only the
shabbiest clothes from my wardrobe, scarcely using soap and
toothpaste and often no deodorant, to be as 'roots' and
natural as my brethren. Concerned, obviously, she must have
been, also as to how this new me would impact on her friends
and family. Worried also was she that I must have gone out of
my mind. How could this man, whom she had so loved and

married for his dynamism, professionalism, potential, ambition and desire for upward mobility, so turn back and become a Rasta of all things? Those things happened only to the next person and affected you directly only in respect of evoking from you sympathy and temporary sorrow for that person. But here it was unfolding in her own life and in absolute reality, for this certainly was no dream.

Unlike his usually impressive and salesman-slick deportment, his hair is now usually uncombed and that on his face so unattractively unkempt with his usually glistening white teeth now showing signs of stains. But most befuddling is the fact that he seems not to care. Where the hell will this all lead to? must have been one of her more serious ruminations.

Never one to give up, she invited the pastor to meet and discuss religion with me in the hope of channelling my obvious passion to a more acceptable religious outlet. The pastor and I reasoned for a long time, but I was too far gone for recall, and when he spoke of King David and Emperor Haile Selassie disparagingly, he alienated me so totally that he thereafter reasoned to deaf ears.

One thing seemed evident from the meeting, and it was that I had wasted all of my earlier years living and being part of a religious lie. As Bob Marley sang, 'I felt like bombing a church now that I knew the preacher was lying'.

Yes, our young marital relationship was suffering from a serious case of 'shell shock' and the inseparable closeness that had characterised it had cracked somewhat, as I became a distinctly different person. 'When and where will this nightmare end?' I am sure she asked herself. I, on the other hand, had found God and knew there was simply no turning back, and prepared myself to walk, sacrificially, the road wherever it led and face the consequences whatever they were.

Still, she was always a faithful and devoted woman, and remained so in spite of the new predicament.

My father, especially, and my stepmother had, over the years, been so proud of my progress in my chosen career, proud of me also from the standpoint that I was always there for them and willing to help in any way I could. Now they were flabbergasted. They simply could not understand how I, of all persons, could succumb to such a reversal. How could such an evil befall me? Worse, they realised they could do nothing to change my mind.

Deep down I sorrowed for them, but the truth was they were a part of this unreasonable and untruthful system that had, heretofore, unwittingly or not, suppressed the real truth, probably because it was not consistent with their preferred social structure. Nonetheless, as a son, I really sorrowed for my father when he accompanied me to my 'farm' and witnessed me working the field, barefooted as a common labourer, similar to those he used to employ. The restrained tears in his eyes said it all: namely, in spite of all this better education he had helped to give me, I had now fallen a generation behind. He, a seasoned farmer, started to criticise my farming techniques, stating that nothing would come of my efforts doing it this way. Then a miracle unfolded in front of my very eyes. Tomato seeds previously planted, with no visible sign of growth, just seemed to burst forth in front of our very eyes. He had to concede that, to that point, my efforts were not in vain.

My older brother, my mentor prior to Ringo, and one of my proudest fans, regretted the day he had introduced me to Ringo. How could I have allowed Ringo to haul me into this Rasta foolishness? He was the one who came around most, trying to unconvert me. Instead I tried to convert him and save his soul, and when he resisted conversion in his intolerant ways I thought of him as spiritually blind and lost.

My younger brother must have been so very hurt by this inexplicable move of mine. He had literally idolised me, seeing me as that star that would make the family name mean something. When the media carried my name for some real estate accomplishment, or there was a favourable write-up for the band, or when he toured with my disco and we had the audience in our hands, his face mirrored greater satisfaction even than mine. His bigger brother, me, was what he hoped to be like. This retrograde step must have hit him as hard as when Mama had died, he being the sole one remaining at home and but nine years of age. I had seen him through tertiary college whilst he lived with me as a bachelor, and when I took to myself a bride he also lived with us. Now I had turned a Rasta, of all things.

Had I known then the full extent of the impact on those close to me, I might have deliberated yet longer but I would still have acceded to what I perceived to be a compelling call from God, and indeed what was to be had to be.

My sisters, too, were concerned, but being more philosophically inclined, they were not so intolerant of my choice of direction and I, in fact, managed to get one to read the Bible, a chapter a day, in search of the truth concerning the Twelve Tribes of Israel. In due time she 'stepped up', taking her place in the house as a sister of the tribe of Reuben.

My employers realised, as I did on 'stepping up', that my chosen religion and the job just did not mix well, so when I submitted my resignation plus a drafted recommendation for the managing director's signature, there were no pleas for its withdrawal.

The group of budding lawyers and executives with whom I

previously drank weekly surprised me with their lack of complaisance and subjected my 'truth' and myself to ridicule, even declining my invitation for a drink at my recently purchased home. As the leading figure said sarcastically, disparagingly, 'We fear you may convert us'.

This reaction, among other things, led my basically shy personality to wonder how my closer friends felt, deep down, about continued relationship. I certainly knew Rasta was absolutely unglamorous socially, to put it mildly. I quite frankly didn't know if they wanted me polluting their space with my presence. I decided to keep my distance and kept to it; so did they, most of them anyway. Probably they too thought I didn't wish their Babylonian presence polluting my space, I now contemplate in hindsight.

Thereafter, I spoke to none from the 'old world' unless they indicated that they wished to converse with me. Some, like a cousin, came by to claim things of mine no longer relevant to my lifestyle like my *Playboy* and *Penthouse* magazines. One or two did come genuinely to keep in touch and see how we were coping. One did come, though, to see if he could invite my wife's embrace from me to him.

My wife's friends came to see if she was okay.

Her mother and father concealed their hurt well, but when, later, a cousin of my wife, living with them, saw the light and came into it, their armour was broken and one could sense and see their pain. Like pleasure, though, pain is part of life.

Being a very, very private person, my deepest thoughts and emotions are seldom shared with anyone, sometimes not even my wife – although we were, most times, almost inseparably close. I remember as a child having a worrying bump on my penis and not finding it possible to share this intimate matter with my mother, and we were quite close also.

When earlier in my conversion, I had experienced inexplicable supernatural (as they seemed to me) situations, I did not share these even with my wife, just as I hadn't shared with her my first traumatic experience of herb smoking or how terrified, lonely and helpless I felt on encountering this surprising change of direction in my life.

To my mind, the call was unmistakably from God and if Jonah could not run successfully, neither could I.

Who likes giving up a satisfactory lifestyle to grope in the dark not knowing where exactly the light is or what else awe-inspiring might be lurking there?

Of course, finding God and truth meant a whole lot, but what did I know then of what to expect? The Bible made mention of the little book being sweet to the mouth but bitter to the belly. How often had I read in the Bible of the various trials and tribulations to which the chosen were subjected, throughout thousands of years. Even our wonderful Lord and Saviour was subjected to all sorts of humiliation and brutalities. And, of course, this current system was no different in this regard, they saw us as trash and treated us accordingly. I was literally scared shitless. What the hell had I got myself into? Yet two factors cornered me; firstly, you just simply cannot run and hide from God, and secondly the truth is simply the truth and must be stood up for. I remember the prophet advising, 'Nothing worth dying, then nothing worth living for.'

My next big predicament was how was I going to interact with the brethren, many of whom I was just now meeting, some of whom, unlike the set I had earlier met, being so unwelcoming and so awesome looking. In spite of the prophet's admonition, they weren't exactly prepared to welcome with open arms any uptown baldhead as brethren to them, orthodox, original, roots, dreadlocks Rasta. I realised that a struggle was on hand to get and keep my seat for which I was chosen, and had sacrificed greatly for.

How, also, was I going to cope with the daily shakedown by the police, or the scorn on the face of anyone, almost, whom I encountered, wherever?

It was certainly going to be a rough experience which I knew not where it would lead, though I learnt that we would form the righteous government of God in the last days. But in the meanwhile, everywhere I turned, prickle stuck me!

I metaphorically, as also literally, felt born again: literally in the sense that I had to start from scratch in finding a way to deal with life anew, with no experience to call on, and this time, with no mother and father! All I had in my camp were my wife, reeling from culture shock tailspin, Ringo, himself trying to find his way, and the prophet to whom I was not yet close.

I now had to dig deep in my resources to find the necessary coping mechanism to deal with this new life as I turned my back on the old life. I tried my best not to concern myself with what they were saying about me within and without the 'house', as I sought to find out what was my role within the House of Israel, and approached this with characteristic passion and commitment, probably too much.

Having eventually overcome the fear relating to my first experience, I now considered the herb part and parcel of the religion, and saw the substance as a useful God-given tool in containing, constraining, even banishing, my fears, my tremors, my inhibitions. So I leaned on the herb heavily, to help me face the day, to help me face the offending brethren, to help me face the 'Babylonians'.

Being a natural worrier, I feared developing this great reliance on the herb only to find that it became unavailable. I also feared consuming too much, hence venturing mentally too far into the unknown. In this regard, as in most others, I called upon my new-found faith in God as I faced up to and embarked on my new life as a revived spirit of the House of the Twelve Tribes of Israel, a chosen of Jah from the tribe of Naphtali.

Economically, I had a little money in the bank, a few receivables, interest in three residential lots in partnership with Ringo, my home on mortgage, and part-interest, along with Ringo, in the fifty acres of agricultural land.

My wife had a reasonable job, but I had no real inflow source; yet, somehow I just did not consider my future economic situation as being as precarious as it actually was. Somehow, not having a job was not as worrying as it should have been. The effects of the herb must have been working too well in dulling my cares and concerns, to the extent that an unjustified sense of security must have set in. I just don't remember being concerned, as I should have been, by the absence of a real source of income. Maybe I was getting mad, damn mad enough to think that, starting from scratch and with no real practical experience in the field, Ringo and myself could make the agricultural land viable, and would achieve this without loan capital (there being no title to the holding to pledge as security.

Nonetheless, I visited the farming store and bought up my stocks of the best farming implements, forks, spades, hoes, machetes, files, budding knives. I then arranged for the five acres which were easily accessible to be ploughed, made the mistake of paying the tractor owner in advance and, as a result, had to visit him at his home early mornings to threaten him before the job was completed, to a degree. I had embarked on the major task of getting the entire fifty acres under control and had employed a commissioned land surveyor to identify the boundaries whilst the workmen with the fence posts followed behind in his footsteps. The project had to be abandoned midway as the squatters on the north-western boundary resisted strongly and relentlessly, with machetes in hand. The fence posts erected to that point soon disappeared, as did my capital, with not much of productive benefit accomplished.

I, then, for the time being, moved my focus to the five acres whilst Ringo tried to open up a larger tract of the land by bulldozing a road separate from the one I accessed my five acres from. In time, his road would connect the tract I was working and a substantial portion of the land would be opened up. Thereafter, we could address the matter of the squatters on the boundary.

This road, apart from opening up acres of good arable land, would also provide access to five lovely hills from which a beautiful view of Kingston city unfolded. How wonderful of Jah, I thought, to have made Ringo and myself custodian of this holding which would one day house so many of my brethren and sisters, in peace and harmony and security and comfort. The prophet would have the first choice of which hill to build his home on, Judah would have the next and I one of the remaining. In the meanwhile, I would get my five acres going in a manner worthy of praise from the prophet, Judah, the brethren and sisters, as the recognition of my usefulness within the house would become more clear to one and all. And jointly with my work in helping the cricket in the house, I might just win a place of acceptance as a respected prince of the tribe of Naphtali. This is how I started thinking as I sought out, more and more, better quality of herb to give me a better high as I embarked on the process of making my vineyard a showpiece.

Prior to my conversion, my brothers and I had attempted an agricultural food distribution business pursuant on which we had gathered extensive information, via questionnaires, in respect of people's preferences in relation to agricultural foodstuff. Now I spent nights, alone, going through these thousands of questionnaires, trying to establish the precise percentage preference of each item in order to utilise the plot of land proportionately optimally. I made a map to scale, bearing the precise dimensions of the lot, and thereafter allocated, exactly, the area for each crop, relative to the findings of my 'land use survey' based on the questionnaire responses. So focused was I on being precisely correct on how the five acres was to be agriculturally subdivided, so engrossed in this tedious exercise, that I somehow lost all track of the fact that it was all an exercise in futility, for indeed, the theory was pointless as the little tract could have been planted out in almost any of the crops in any ratio. Somehow my thinking had become foolishly logical, awfully impractical and irrelevantly focused, as the herb became more and more a constant companion and adviser. In hindsight, I now realise I must have started losing sanity from the time – or even before – I started using the herb too regularly.

The entire farming project was draining more and more of our financial resources. Ringo joined, enthusiastically, the squander-mania as he hurriedly bulldozed chains of road-way, which, left unpaved, became a conduit for water flooding out people's houses on both sides when it rained.

I, in the meanwhile, was journeying the thirty-odd miles daily, and sometimes more often, with material and labour, not even realising how uneconomical the whole project was.

How had I, a top sales producer, become such an idiot businesswise and otherwise, such a fool that, apart from making a mess of this farming initiative, I also continued to think Ringo Judah knew what he was doing and confidently supported him as I always did? To be honest, although there was an economic angle to the project, a primary focus was the provision of food for God's people, but we certainly were not going about it efficiently and sensibly.

My wife was always a level headed young woman; consequently, it is easily understood that acceptance of my new-found truth was not forthcoming and when I offered her a taste of the wisdom-giving herb it was angrily refused, much to my annoyance.

Why, I thought to myself, couldn't she come down off her pomp and pride and see Jah light?

We therefore soon started to grow apart as I, my doctrine, dress and general deportment became less and less tolerable and presentable and my herb-smoking habit escalated significantly.

I knew I had been 'called' and I knew I had found truth. I had also read that one had to be prepared to give up all, if necessary, in order to take up the cross. Additionally, I had heard or read that one would be considered mad for having taken up the cross, as many were now, I was sure, considering me. I decided that 'que sera, sera', though I still invited my wife to start reading her Bible seriously, and explained to her all I had learnt regarding the Twelve Tribes of Israel, the same people she was reading of in the Bible, but now revived, in this time, under this risen prophet of God. In time I also invited her to our public meetings. Eventually, at last, she decided not to leave me but to 'step up' and join me in the house of Israel as a sister of the tribe of Dan. Soon after, the female cousin of hers, living in her mother's house, did likewise.

As for the commercial band, Ringo had decreed that we would no longer be a dance band playing all types of music, but a Rasta reggae show band playing just Rasta reggae music, this in the time when king Marley was conquering the earth with the same music.

Still, this predominantly drum and bass idiom was not yet within the boys' level of excellence and, quite frankly, this was not attractive to the clientele we had built up over the years.

Twelve Tribes, too, had had their own band and a host of singers and players; however, they had no equipment. Ringo Judah, to much applause on the Hill, donated the band's equipment, our equipment, to the 'organ'.

Soon, our band, within the top three popular bands nationally, faded from the commercial scene to play, along with the Twelve Tribes' band, principally within the house, venturing out for a gig only occasionally, usually displeasing the patrons with too much Rasta reggae music.

4

The Doctrine, The Movement, The Chosen, The Commitment, The Herb

As I understood it from the Bible, God, seeing Abraham a most good and righteous man, decided to breed from his seed a people special to Him, the Almighty. This, His promise to Abraham, was not manifested in his time though the promise was restated to Isaac, Abraham's son, but was not manifested in his time. In Jacob, the next generation, the promise was fulfilled and his name changed to Israel and his twelve sons became the foundation, the patriarchs of the twelve tribes of Israel, a people especial to God and one through whom other nations would be blessed. Israel had, also, one daughter, Dinah.

The reading of the Scriptures indicated undoubtedly, to me, that they were primarily and predominantly about those people the Israelites, something my earlier association with the Bible and church had not even hinted at; in fact, all I had thought I knew about the contents of the Bible before proved to be nought. As a result of this revelation, this soul stirring knowledge, I embarked even more vigorously in further Bible study.

The organ required that every member read a chapter a day, progressively, starting from Genesis 1, whilst studying the Good Book generally, seriously. Most of us did so obsessively. The exhortation was towards reading the Scriptures for yourself, unearthing your own truths instead of depending on a religious leader to read and interpret for you. We were taught that the words of the Bible spoke directly to the spirit of each of us in a manner individually appropriate, relevant and beneficial.

The children of Israel multiplied tremendously and became a powerful nation but they were inclined to be stiff-necked and often disobedient to their God. As a result of their frequent misbehaviour, Jehovah, their God, turned his back on them from time to time, and finally scattered them far and wide, subjecting them to all sorts of hardships in strange lands all over the globe; scattered but not forgotten forever.

Now in this time, my time, came a prophet, as of old, to raise up the spirits of these mighty people, many resident in Jamaica, by leading them into the Bible and showing them their rich heritage and future victory guaranteed.

The spirit of the prophet, I learnt, came alive with the Emperor of Ethiopia visiting Jamaica, identifying himself, to him, as the Conquering Lion of the Tribe of Judah, instructing him to organise and centralise and making him the present of a watch, symbolic of the Twelve Tribes. He, the prophet, was the first dry bone being brought back to life and to service in the revival of the house of Israel, starting with the island of Jamaica.

The Emperor being on that throne and lineage dating back to King Solomon, and being therefore a direct descendant of

King David and likewise of Jesus Christ, was worshipped as the living God, God with us, being the returned Messiah, Christ in His kingly character, earth's rightful ruler.

The prophet got the call. Thereafter, after going through the Bible with a fine-tooth comb, learning the fullness of his mission, he took to the streets with his message, firstly working towards finding the first twelve, the executives, plus a sister, representative of the children of Israel. Each of the twelve had to be from a different tribe, the tribe being indicated by the month in which one was born. If close to the end of the month, further research relative to the location of the moon at the date of birth would determine the specific tribe.

Each tribe represented a different part of the Body of Christ and bore various different characteristics; and each had received different blessings from Israel, their father, and later, from Moses the prophet, of a later dispensation.

These were the Twelve Tribes of which twelve thousand of each would be sealed for the righteous government of God in these last days.

The first born was Reuben, April born represented by the eyes, mighty and excellent but unstable as water. Simeon represented by the ears and Levi the nose were characterised by their anger. The Levites, nonetheless, were the ones chosen for priestly duties, then and now. May and June were their months respectively.

Judah, the fourth, July born, represented by the mouth/heart is 'he whom his brethren shall praise and the sceptre shall not depart from Judah until Shiloh comes.' Issachar, the hands, August, is a strong ass. Zebulun the belly, September, shall dwell at the haven of the sea. Dan, October, the back, shall judge his people. Gad, November, the pelvic region, shall be overcome but shall overcome at last. Asher, December, the thigh, his bread shall be fat and he will yield royal dainties. Naphtali, the knee, my tribe, January born, is 'like a hind let loose giving goodly words.' Joseph, February, the calf is a fruitful bough, shot at but blessed and strengthened by the hands of the Almighty, he is a most favoured. Benjamin, the foot, March born, the last born of the twelve shall in the morning devour the prey and at night divide the spoil.

One's tribe determined one's dominant characteristics and was a guide to others as to how to relate to that brethren or sister and to the roles he or she was best suited for.

After the first twelve elders and the sister representative, Dinah, were found, an executive of sisters was similarly established.

At my time of entry into the movement, the first and second executive elders of male and female were already established. There was a couple of thousand more of us, members, recorded in the book of life.

The first convert of the prophet, as he had started out on his mission, was a Naphtalite who therefore assumed the role as Naphtali first. They both started paying dues at that time, with each being custodian of the funds on alternative weeks. These I learnt from the meetings on the hill.

These dues would be used to take care of the business of the organisation and in time were the basis of financing the repatriation of brethren to Africa, motherland, and, more particularly, Ethiopia, homeland. In time we would all be repatriated, initially occupying lands His Majesty was said to have earmarked for us.

The organisation was founded and maintained on Rastafarian principles and beliefs and unapologetically recognised Africa as our real roots and Ethiopia as the destination of our repatriation; however, anyone of any colour or race was welcome and it was not mandatory that one be 'dreadlocked' in hair, as to be 'dread' in heart was more important. The prophet himself, in fact, did not wear his hair in dreadlocks, probably to emphasise the point. Other branches of Rastafarians and even some of our members frowned upon the act of dilution of Rasta practices.

In my time, all colours and races were present within the organisation, the majority dreadlocked, but quite a few not so.

The first appeal of the prophet, on assuming his mission, was, I learnt, to existing Rastas who, before the prophet's call had been serving and worshipping the Ethiopian king from his coronation in 1930. Some heeded the call, others remained in or joined other branches, some joined none but saw not this doctrine as authentic. Many, at the time of my involvement, even criticised with 'blood and fire' the 'organ' in respect of its policies, particularly those of classifying 'baldheads' as Rasta and also those relating to its admittance of other than black people, 'uptowners' even, into the ranks of Rastafari. Some made it quite plain to the likes of me that we were impostors not even prepared to take the Nazarite vow, grow our locks and thereby relinquish our safe haven in Babylon. I had sacrificed much to be a part of this movement, but I realised many, even within the house, would never accept me as genuine Rasta.

Many existing Rastas did not heed the prophet's call, being too rebellious in spirit, they simply were not going to deal with anything requiring them to join up or line up.

From the word go, the prophet encountered a 'fight' from many foundational Rastas especially, and of course he was considered mad by most other persons, as, by the street side, he peddled his message then, concerning the revival of the house of Israel, the dry bones returned to life.

The membership of the organisation met once every month religiously, rain or sunshine, at different places, but had, during my time, graduated to the Hill as permanent home. The Hill was located a few miles out of town in a north-eastern direction.

The prophet, too, at my time of joining, had been forced out of his ghetto location by political and other Babylonian interests, and thereafter abode at Rastaman's Heights, a less dangerous type of depressed community.

Dues were paid elsewhere, at an elder's home, but a steady stream of brothers and sisters like myself would visit the prophet at his home to enquire at his feet concerning many things and to see to his general well being. For myself I always approached him in awe, befitting his status, as I saw it then.

The dues, in my time, were twenty cents per week and it did seem miraculous to me that this was the financial basis, pledges also, on which the necessaries of the house, including the purchase and maintenance of a vehicle, were met. And there was never a child born in the house, including mine, to whose parent a cash gift was not made. Out of the resources also, were airline tickets bought to send brethren to the land, Ethiopia. It seemed miraculous to me, then and now, but their financial and other planning was simply ingenious.

The prophet, the spiritual leader and chief in all other regards was the force around which everything happened. He it is who was recognised by almost the entire membership as having the direct line to the Almighty and he it is who dispensed God's instructions to the membership. He was also the main target of opposition from the government, the system, angry parents and relatives of members, and even within the house I later found out, existed pockets of disgruntled brethren and sisters. But a wise, cunning, tough, compassionate, crafty, shrewd, frugal, kind, rough, focused opponent he was to all comers. He was loved, feared, respected, almost worshipped by almost all of us within the house. He possessed an abnormally outstanding focal ability and an ingenious sense of comprehension and retention of information.

One of the principles we were taught was 'one for all and all for one'; in this manner there would be no failure. This, he said, was one of the principles of our functioning, passed down by His Majesty. We all, almost, lived this principle and benefited from it singly and mutually.

Money, he preached, has a way of creating confusion and rift, especially among poor people, so any time there was too much lying idle in the consolidated fund some useful purpose was found to absorb it.

Most of us who had had a taste of some money soon despised the commodity and spent freely, benevolently, almost seeking to rid ourselves of that 'evil', filling the void instead with good deeds and other acts toward spiritual development.

Nonetheless, some saw us uptown 'baldheads' as spies and opportunists from the system, bent on exploiting whatever business opportunities existed within the membership. Most of us so categorised went overboard in acts of generosity to erode this perception. What the prophet said privately to our accusers I don't know, but publicly he defended us stoutly, even to mentioning, on the Hill, the great contribution of the newcomers to the organisation.

Discipline was never compromised within the house, as I saw it, and seemed to be upheld strongly at all times.

These, the membership, were primarily men and women of awe-inspiring dread, often hungry, disfranchised, oppressed, angry, ready to explode. A firm hand had to be employed, by the prophet especially, at all times, to hold it all together, and it had in fact taken a great deal of firm control to build the movement and have it progress to this stage. Coming from where I was socially, and to anyone else unfamiliar to Rasta, some of the brothers and sisters bore an appearance, mannerism and way of speech that would make you want to flee their presence if encountered in the night or in the day. And they were all so militantly angry with anything representative of the Babylonian system, even a person properly dressed. The membership consisted of many of these, so the hands of the prophet had to be firm, very firm, to keep things in check. Any act like thieving, lying, thoughtlessness, brethren to brethren, was scorned and offenders were dealt with quite severely on the Hill. To be called up in front of the brethren for an infraction was definitely one of the worst things that could ever happen to a member. A brethren striking another meant suspension, even excommunication, and that was a fate almost like death to a serious Israelite. As a result of such a conviction, even friends treated the convicted as a pariah and we all knew that the protection and guidance of the Almighty, also, left such a one. That person would be all alone, out in the cold, to face the numerous daily trials and tribulations, without the united strength of the house or the mighty hand of the Almighty God.

Talk about commitment to duty. If you were assigned a task, you were expected to accomplish it, with no excuse being good enough. To me newly out of 'Babylon' I was just now understanding what real commitment meant, for indeed the level I was accustomed to before was not that much by comparison.

With everyone programmed to accomplish at all cost, little excuses like rain pouring and or no bus running or illness would certainly be ridiculed, for even if your feet were your only carriage then the assignment was to be accomplished. And to fail the organ usually meant being called up in front of the membership on the Hill to face the wrath of the prophet, the elders and the entire membership inclusive of the friends if the matter was serious enough. Minor matters, the prophet dealt with from his home base.

In one's own sphere one could be the toppest notch, but in relation to the business of the house, none amongst us was bigger than the humblest in terms of rights and privileges. This in reality was not exactly totally and entirely so, but, to me, seemed so to a commendable extent, especially in the light of the partiality and prejudices I had lived with within the outside world.

We were also taught that everything was to be done in a disciplined and orderly manner, everything. Confusion, the prophet preached constantly, was a product of the devil, the opponent.

The principle of divide and rule was what the existing political system was based on: consequently, we were not to involve ourselves in that process, and we, almost all, did not participate in elections, though, in prudence, it was good to seek an amicable relationship with all and sundry.

Bible reading was a must for everyone, that being the way to feed the spirit, to development. A chapter a day progressively was mandatory, and most of us, additionally, devoured all areas of the Scriptures daily, considering ourselves perpetual students of the Bible.

Marcus Garvey was accepted, without doubt as the prophet prior to our current one, and though it was not mandatory, a true Israelite hungrily sought his teachings. As a consequence pamphlets were readily available, on sale from brethren, at low cost.

Most ate 'ital': no salt, and in many cases no meat. Still others like myself had non-ital food with the exception of pork and other 'unclean' foods which were absolutely taboo. This reasonable freedom in cuisine was singular to this branch of Rastafarian, as most others held very strict eating habits and criticised Twelve Tribes strongly on this point of liberality also. The members of the other branches as well as some foundation Rastas within the house, did not allow their 'queens' to handle food during menstruation, and if pork was cooked from a pot they would not eat from that pot ever again. While, however, the others were criticising and adhering to all sorts of writs and rites and isms and schisms, Twelve Tribes was expanding in all areas, socio-economically and into foreign lands as complete executives were being seated in various countries including England and the United States. Also, brethren were being repatriated to Ethiopia not infrequently and residing on the land provided by His Majesty.

Jesus Christ, to almost all of us, was the undoubted Messiah of old, the Son of God, the Miracle Maker, the Teacher, the Preacher, the Sacrificial Lamb begotten and beloved of God and us. Some 'dreads' who had stepped into the organ from some other Rastafarian branches did not accept Jesus in any respected capacity, just like a rebellious few did not respect the Bible as a scriptural authority. To them His Imperial

Majesty Haile Selassie the First was the beginning, the middle and the end.

The vast majority of the membership, though, worshipped His Majesty as Jesus Christ returned in His kingly character and he was worshipped by one and all as the Mighty God who had chosen and called all of us to a higher life.

I simply had not in my life or dreams to date seen any reverence similar to how this stern-faced being was loved and adored and worshipped, in absentia, as our God. He was truly revered by one and all.

Often you hailed a brethren with the words 'Selassie I' to which he may respond 'Mighty God, earth's rightful ruler' or simply, 'Guidance and protection', or similarly, 'Selassie I'.

Seldom would a good Israelite attempt anything significant before giving thanks to the King of Kings and Lord of Lords, the Conquering Lion of the tribe of Judah, elect of God, Light of this world, earth's rightful ruler, His Imperial Majesty, Emperor Haile Selassie the First. A good Israelite, certainly I, travelled with His Majesty in mind constantly, day and night, always seeking how to please him. And in my workroom/ study the walls were lined with pictures of and literature on him, as were the homes of most Israelites.

Where we managed to get all these books and pictures of him I don't know, but his picture was absolutely everywhere, within our circle, hundreds of pictures.

Soon after joining the organisation, I gave him my absolute allegiance, even to the cost of my life and, through my eyes, it seemed as if the majority of the brethren were similarly committed.

If indeed, as I now thought, I housed the spirit of an Israelite of old, now revived in this time, being one of but a couple thousand similarly called to date, then I was certainly chosen and handpicked by the Almighty God or his assigned angels, to be one of the foundation pillars on which his righteous government would be founded. This was really heavy, heady stuff, for indeed my name would surely be already entered in the Lamb's Book of Life. All I had to do, therefore, was to continue on track, performing as a devoted, dedicated productive child of God and eternal life would be mine: indeed, I would have overcome the world, reaping just rewards for the sacrifices I was prepared to and did make. This being so, entry into the Twelve Tribes of Israel was by far the best move I could ever have made.

The Bible and all else I read depicted the measureless power of the Almighty, and when I saw in the Scriptures where He, personally, with His hosts, fought wars on behalf of His chosen people, annihilating the opposition, and when I read how He had personally selected this people to be His very own via Father Abraham, then Isaac, making us a reality in Jacob, Israel, and realised that we now were the dry bones of that people now brought back to life, I could scarcely take it in. I, simple me, was one of the chosen and God the Almighty, the Creator, was almost literally my Father and I was one of his children. I felt special, chosen, victorious, triumphant, protected, guaranteed, a stake holder; though I was still somewhat awed by the trials and tribulations that I, we, would have to bear here on earth, in our day-to-day existence.

There was also the stress associated with the question of whether I would be able to live up full enough to satisfy this most Almighty of beings in whose spotlight I was now focused, and although I knew His Son, Jesus Christ, in His first coming had died for our sins, I was very apprehensive about my sins of the past and somehow felt I had to over-compensate for them to be blotted out.

The closer I got to the prophet, as in time I did, the more I felt I was under the microscope of the Almighty who had given me this new opportunity to come good enough to erase the errors of the past. And as a chosen plucked from a comfortable middle-income sphere, a situation so unlike where the majority came from, I figured I was called for a special role and as the prophet often quoted, 'To whom much is given, much is required'.

My role wasn't, I reasoned, in the area of music, as was the case of most of the brethren who were singers and players of instruments. My role, I thought, had to do with leadership, management, growth, example, structuring and, of course, escalated development of the sport of cricket within the house. Oh how I welcomed this opportunity to maximise, in an exemplary impressive way, the talent in the sport which I had failed to develop fully. And how my dreamer's heart saw our team rising to great heights nationally. And how, I dreamt on, further afield, to the time when I would be instrumental in staging the Israel games, among the tribes, at the National Stadium with the television cameras recording it all for the country and later the world to see the chosen of God in good spirited but keen rivalry and revelry thereafter. All this in time.

The games would encompass tests of skill in all the sports active in the house. I could just see myself, probably team captain for the tribe of Naphtali, resplendent in my green outer suit whilst the other tribes were similarly in their various tribe colours, as we displayed ourselves in the open-ing ceremony. In spite of the trials and tribulations, I mused, the true me not yet seen will truly find my days of glory ... in time.

Though my mortal side still feared death, theoretically I knew that, despite my promiscuous past, now as a chosen, death had no dominion over me having found the road to eternal life. I merely had to live upfull and excel at my given role to claim that prize.

Prior to conversion, when I did pray, I had not the faith that those words would possibly find their way to the Almighty, the Creator; now I had no doubt that the prayers of us, the chosen, would surely reach his ears and, in time, I knew that 'He shall give His angels charge over thee to keep thee in all thy ways.' As a chosen, I understood, it was given to us to perform, with faith, works similar to that which the great Jesus Christ had accomplished. Still the human in me often trembled at the numerous trials and tribulations lurking ahead, foretold and unforetold.

My search, prior to conversion, had been motivated, primarily, by the question, Why did so many of us, not necessarily good, have so much, whilst some had so little? Now having found God I continued my ponderings on another question: Why are some chosen and so many others overlooked? My naïve mind just wanted to know that justice and fair play were inherent in the process. In time, I accepted the fact that God knows best, appreciated my good luck, and put my shoulder to the wheel, helping to structure the army for Armageddon and thereafter the establishment of the righteous government of God. This was the level of thinking that now characterised my person.

Indeed, I took to my perceived duty with great passion, more even than before for; to my mind, this work was not of or for man, but in the service of the Almighty God.

Scripturally, others read their chapter once daily, some having difficulty in so doing; I read mine seven times at one sitting before food didst touch my mouth. I sought, by so doing, to extract every morsel of understanding from every word I read in that chapter. And as a separate exercise, I daily devoured volumes elsewhere in the Holy Bible.

In the cricket arena, especially in the second year, I sought to develop exemplary competence, attitude, deportment and bearing in order to shine a positively impressive light, to onlookers, towards influencing them to the God I served. At worst, I wanted them to see Rastafarians in a better light and form a better impression of us. I started now to attire myself more impressively on and off the field, with my banner on my head identifying me with the organ. To escalate my performance at the sport, I made best use of each training session, whilst, as a separate exercise, I ran nine miles daily. Previously I had had difficulty completing one quarter of a mile. It certainly worked for me; I found real fitness and this transformed my on-the-field performance, batting, bowling or fielding to unquestionable excellence.

In time I became vice-captain and executive member of the cricket board. Our beloved captain had passed on and the then vice-captain assumed his place. The captain had passed on tragically, but not before he had told me, in the presence of another, that he had observed me from when I stepped up and knew I was there to perform a great work.

I now used our daily practices and weekly meetings as a forum to lift the others up to the desired commitment, befitting and necessary, in the name of Jah, Rastafari; God's new name in this time, a name at which the heathen trembled.

Where we had our cricket practice and where the band

rehearsals were held were close to each other, so I passed by rehearsals, to look in on those brethren and help however I could. Ringo was not much of a reader, so I would interpret for him what was embodied in the books on the business of music.

I still had a car (later, only access to one), but I assumed a role of transporter, assisting brethren and sisters from place to place benevolently. In time, as I got closer and closer to the prophet, I became sort of unofficially one of his chauffeurs, willing to take him anywhere he wished, including some real criminally and politically tense inner city locations.

My wife and I hosted, at our home, the first-ever party for all executives, first and second elders, male and female, within the organisation. This was not long after we had joined the organisation, and at a time when the third executives had not yet been seated; so every sitting executive-elder of God was actually feted under our roof. Some of these elders were entering in this type of home for the first time in their lives and made good use of the delectables as all had a deservedly good time. And being matched, though not conclusively, to the tribe of Naphtali, I, thereafter, sought at every occasion to be of material assistance to the Naphtali first elders, male and female, people of very meagre and humble means. When the Danite elder, the male elder of my wife's tribe, passed early in the morning on his newspaper route I was up to greet him with a hot cup of tea and an orange. And whatever I had I was prepared to freely share with my brethren and sisters as I decided to live in reality the pentecostal spirit of sharing and caring as I interpreted it from the Acts of the Apostles. Even some lovely pictures of His Majesty, which I had purchased, I freely shared with my brethren. And I certainly was not sparing to them with gifts of food and even intangibles like encouragement and love. A paraplegic brethren, especially, I was very supportive of, always being there for him however often he needed my help.

Quite often, brethren were incarcerated, often unjustifiably, sometimes for herb, which we, incidentally, considered unjust to be locked up for. There were others who were more often called on to bail them, but in this area I was also called on. I remember a member of the cricket team being locked up for herb and I was so disappointed when neither the manager nor the captain nor any other was showing any interest in offering assistance, because they said the brethren should have known better than to smoke on the road – something, incidentally, we all did.

I got a recommendation from an ex-magistrate, attesting to my trustworthiness and soon used this to get him out.

I did truly hate this type of interaction with the law, of which I was terribly afraid but found myself having to bail brethren from time to time, though not frequently.

My home was now like a refuge for many brethren and sisters who came by for various types of help, and my wife, being a good woman, supported me in offering a helping hand however we could, she doing so in a manner not impractical to our own personal needs.

And when I reaped from my farm, I sold nought, but filled my barns and gave the remainder to many in need.

When I decide to commit, I, often unwisely, do so with my heart, soul, body and mind, with almost foolish limitlessnes. This time, however, I knew I was doing so in the work of my new-found God, so I extended myself more fully, without regret.

In this manner, I approached my commitment to duty, prepared to face death even, for this cause.

If it were not for my wife's restraining hand, I might have given away almost everything. Somehow, I must already have lost track of reality.

Why was Babylon so bent on stamping out the use of the herb when one was free to drink all the alcohol one wished? We reasoned that they, being under satanic government, wanted to deny us of that which awakened our spirits to our rich heritage of true children of God. They wanted to deny us that which made us reason and focus beyond the day-to-day slavery routine. They certainly did not want us to find the truth and our Maker, whereby we would unify ourselves towards that Armageddon, towards that victory, towards peace on earth, towards that righteous government under the Almighty. 'The kings of the earth set themselves and the rulers take counsel together against the Lord and against His anointed saying let us break their bands asunder...'

For almost all my life, I had had trembling hands, questionable courage and unsure bearing Now, at last, I had found something nicer, less nauseous, more laughter-inspiring than alcohol, that made me calm, courageous, confident even, so I used it to brace and bolster my frail being to do what I perceived had to be done, and I praised my God for having provided it. And did He provide it! I had but to wish for a good 'draw' and someone passed by to fulfil my wishes. Still, this might not have been as miraculous as it seemed, for indeed many of the brethren passed through my home quite regularly, and almost all, besides my wife and a few others, smoked and had it on their person constantly.

The herb also had a way of lifting you into a deep, deep state of meditation, to the extent that I was often reasoning with and hearing the voice of my Father God, or so it seemed.

And the music, the conversation, the food, the sex, the every-thing, just seemed so much more enjoyable in a state of high; everything seemed so amusing, despite existing problems, that laughter and joy came very readily. Then, I knew not that this state could be achieved without this stimulant. I had now begun to enjoy and love the herb very much ... very, very, much.

Many brethren, particularly vendors of the herb, informed me of the numerous judges, lawyers, doctors, policemen, businessmen, politicians who privately used it. Naive me was really shocked.

Brethren also told me that King Solomon, they had read somewhere, had been a constant user of it, hence his great wisdom. In fact, they said, it still grew unabated on his grave. And of course, I said to myself, my brethren in God would not lie or talk foolishness.

In time, I learnt that there is herb and there is herb, and that which I was getting mostly, at the outset, was referred to as 'bush'. As I got more grounded within the organisation, I got exposed to the real 'sweet' genuine 'lamsbread, sensamania, collie herb' which took you on a direct flight to heaven, mentally.

In time, I became so dependent on the herb that I fell in love with it and used it to relax, before meals, before sex, after sex, before, during and after meetings, at band practice, before reading the Bible, having a beer, on the toilet seat and all times in between. I finally fell madly in love ... with the herb, a gift from God to the Rastaman.

5

Guilt, Trials, Tribulations, Intimidation and Me the Fool

I was a converted man but one with quite a guilt complex, a terrible one as a direct result of my past lifestyle prior to entering the house of Israel. How could I then, I agonised, having been provided with so much by God, so very much in comparison to so many others, have lost my way so badly, promiscuously especially, direction and values also.

My focus, at the time, had encompassed making money however not too unacceptable, trying to be considered a success by my peers and others, and indulging in extremely licentious behaviour introverted and nervous though I was.

The whole concept of God, pleasing Him, keeping His commandments, had all been divorced from my lifestyle, to too great an extent, somewhere along the way to adulthood. Maybe if Mama had not died so early in my life or if Papa had extended himself more in moulding my character, or maybe if my big sisters weren't so often off the island at such crucial times, my direction and focus might not have gone askew and

I might have kept to the straight and narrow which I learnt of earlier in life.

Still, I was never in the realms of what one would consider a wicked, cruel or evil person. I was far from that, I was simply a misdirected introverted person too engrossed in scheming how to satisfy my excessive sexual desires. In those early twenties, prior to marriage, I indulged myself with women too numerous to mention without discomfort.

In terms of monetary pursuit I could not have been considered dishonest but would certainly tell a 'white lie' or two to close a sale, especially if the deal was beneficial to the prospect also.

Later, now a man converted to truth and right, equality and justice and the Almighty, I regretted my past lifestyle with my customary passion and felt deeply as if I had very much to compensate for. Why did I think my past life such an absolutely sinful one, even now I can't fully understand. Maybe when I considered my past lifestyle of comfort and ease, monetary and sexual pursuit, as against that which the brethren and sisters had been suffering for God, I felt guilty, to an exaggerated proportion. Recently converted, I then knew a little more about God and good. Knowledge about any subject, certainly the Divine, obviously does not come all at once; I had, however, started to read not only of His great love but also of his terrible wrath and his requirement regarding strict adherence to His laws. Chosen or not, I knew I had not lived righteously enough previously, and, to my mind, I had to make amends for those past sins; and did I try, though unsuccessfully, in terms of assuaging my guilt complex. Somehow, my new-found religious knowledge and training had completely excluded the element concerning the forgiving nature of God. Indeed, now in retrospect, I can't remember that aspect of the Creator coming to the fore significantly during my time in the organisation. But then again, it was common knowledge that the Almighty God had sent his only begotten son to suffer on the cross to atone for our sins, epitomising the forgiving nature of God. Somehow I just never inclined my thought in that direction at the time. I suppose it sounded too much like the doctrine I was accustomed to, prior to my involvement in Twelve Tribes. Within the movement, Jesus was known, recognised and respected by most, but only in so far as he had returned in the person of His Imperial Majesty, Haile Selassie I. So, with forgiveness, a distant concept not applicable to me, I submerged my guilt-ridden self in punitive religious work via the organ, Twelve Tribes. The concept of forgiveness absent, I attributed every unpleasant experience that visited me to punishment relative to my dubious past. Some, though, I accepted as the normal trials and tribulations associated with my becoming a Rasta-farian, a disciple of His Imperial Majesty, Haile Selassie I, king of kings, Lord of Lords, conquering lion of the tribe of Judah, our God.

Ganja to us Rastafarians, certainly to my perception, was an integral part of our daily existence and of the worship and praise of our God. A brethren told me that when the psalmist instructed at 24:79 to 'lift up your head oh ye gates', he was referring to the use of herb. The interpretation did not seem all that clear-cut to me, but a seasoned brethren like that, speaking so authoritatively, could hardly be wrong. And there were other scriptural references to the herb that the brethren did point out. And of course, they said, His Majesty God, used it too. The fact that it was against the law of the land was an indication, to others and to me, of the wicked nature of the 'Babylonians' who sought an opportunity to imprison us whilst denying us of that 'brain food' that made us 'know ourselves' and assisted in that meditative contact to our God. In defiance we smoked the herb not only in private, but anywhere the hand of the law could not easily touch us.

Driving in my car I, like the others, in time was enjoying my spliff, my eyes searching the surroundings for any sign of the 'beast' as the police were called.

The prophet's prudent advice on the subject was 'travel with it in your head, not on your person'; surprisingly, nonetheless, we usually travelled with a little stock, and as I said before we defiantly smoked en route driving often enough, travelling on foot, less frequently.

The police, fully aware of our habit, would, as soon as they recognised us as Rasta, stop and search us thoroughly with and total disrespect for our rights as citizens. Herb was not all the police, in protection of the system, had against us. We preached a strange doctrine and philosophy, quite contrary to existing norms. We preached relentlessly for freedom, justice and equality, and in fact agitated quite vociferously for the breaking down of the existing evil system for replacement by a righteous one. We also desired repatriation to Africa our homeland, Ethiopia, the land of our God, and we were generally nonconformist and revolutionary in words, deed and conduct and were facetious enough to refer to them as beasts. There existed a great hate between the police and ourselves. Of course, as in similar situations, I encountered one or two policemen who were sympathetic to our cause or, at least, non-abusive to us. But on a whole, a great misunderstanding widened the chasm between them and us. Except for the defiant use of the herb, a reasonable small infraction, our organisation, and certainly the prophet and the executive, did not advocate breaking the laws of the country. In fact, many a brethren who, prior to membership, would be inclined to be a criminal, would as a member be required to conduct his life in a more exemplary manner. Naturally, there were some not given to any reform, but the majority were peaceful, law abiding, God fearing brothers and sisters seeking only the right to praise their God and, in time, go home to Ethiopia. The authorities, on the other hand, in ignorance, insecurity and fear, saw this gathering of religious militants as a great threat to their safety and governance and directed their security forces at them. The organ fought back the oppression how they could, mostly with words. In time, acrimony turned to hate as the police became more and more abusive. In my time, the existing system was an enemy, especially the police.

A team of police would search any one of us, hoping to find even a seed from the ganja, anywhere on our person, as a basis to lock us up.

Quite a few families, including mine, had lost their beloved children to this movement, to a cult, a prophet, a strange God and a sub-standard lifestyle that had left their 'Christian' hearts broken.

Our movement was therefore not a favourite one of government, families, churches, judges and most definitely not the police. We were despised by all but a few who were brave enough to come close enough to hear that basically what we were advocating, at least vocally, was peace and love, truth and rights, freedom, equality and justice. And there were indeed many within the house who were truly good examples of this.

The politicians hated us because we preached non-involvement in their party politics. Even the poor disliked us, because the poor hate anything that is predominantly poor, financially, is of the poor and peopled by the poor, and that is what the movement was, basically.

I now found myself in a scene almost totally unpopular with all and sundry, and as a consequence was subjected to numerous unaccustomed insults and harassment from the 'Babylonian' side. Trials and tribulations, I said, mixed with punishment for my past sins.

Commercially, I persisted with the 'farm', albeit foolishly and naïvely in approach, to no meaningful avail, economically. Additionally, I embarked on a project of procuring coconuts, then scarce, from the rural areas and converting them to coconut cakes for sale at dances. At other times I 'manufactured' cane juice from the cane at the farm and through purchase from other sources I supplemented my stock of mangoes from the farm for sale at dances and elsewhere. I also procured bananas from a relative, as payment on an old debt, for sale within the house. All these projects, in hindsight, I realise were ill conceived, ridiculously implemented and badly managed.

Missing from my approach was the vital element of profit motivation, then lost in my new money-guilt concept. Still, I would have welcomed some compensating success for all the effort I was putting in; and quite frankly some monetary return, not a lot, would have gone a good way to easing some of my burdens. I had put into the ventures much labour, effort and scarce financial resources, and had reaped, in return, significant losses, much frustration and a good deal of embarrassment. I put it all down to trial and tribulation and punishment for past sins.

I was never one very capable of facing confrontation and defending myself against verbal and other attacks. As a consequence, I had, from youth, absorbed many embarrassing insults silently though seething violently inside.

The membership of the organ had gathered at the airport to send off a brethren to the 'land'. Mission accomplished, we were preparing to depart when a sister beckoned me over. I went, smiling, to her, in response to which she loudly told me, in the hearing of her friends and to the accompaniment of their laughter, to take the smile off my face for she wasn't looking for a man, only a lift home. I, always afraid of embarrassment, slinked away crushed; I could not but think that, in my days of looking for women, she could not, via inner or outer beauty, qualify even to give me a blow job. Remembering that God was privy to every thought of the heart, I repented of this one and all the way home sought his forgiveness for such an evil thought; and against a sister, at that.

I knew that the facetious sister was simply showing off to her friends at my expense, but I also saw her, and the others who insulted me from time to time then, as a vehicle being used by God to punish me for past sins.

Before my 'stepping up', almost all the brethren I had met were accommodating and welcoming; now I was encountering some who clearly thought – and expressed it – that the likes of me had no part in 'their thing' except as purveyors of gifts to their benefit. But then again, I reasoned with myself, I had previously enjoyed a life of plenty, often undeserved, whilst they had been subjected to a miserable existence; therefore it was now their time to have the upper hand in some way. At no time then, strangely enough, did I recognise them for what they were – a worthless set of malcontents standing in the way of persons who wished to do good. Instead, I saw them as part and parcel of my trials and tribulations and punishment, none of which, however, was going to discourage me away from this great calling. In fact, I resolved to be so outstanding an Israelite that even these brethren in my way would, in time, respect me for what I represented. As the prophet often said in his ungrammatical style, having got a seat in the house the responsibly of maintaining it was yours.

Oh, so many trials and tribulations and punishment it all seemed, especially in the early stages. And when Ringo, Judah and I parted company, with the band members siding with him, my punishment seemed so extreme, with me being in this new, mysterious, unfamiliar environment alone – almost entirely so.

I had worked myself up to a position of usefulness to the prophet. On one occasion, I was transporting himself and a sister to an inner city ghetto. Accepting him, as we all do, as God's messenger, the principal one on earth, and knowing that the eyes of God were likely to be on us whilst in his presence, I made sure to avoid all the many potholes lest the ride be too unpleasant for his guest and himself. On reaching the destination, I could not understand the annoyance on their faces as they slammed the car doors so severely. As they departed, I realised what had happened. They had misunderstood my cautious, careful driving as being motivated by my desire to gingerly and frugally preserve the motorcar, and they were angrily showing that it was but a piece of machine. Granted that I must have as usual overdone the whole process, my intentions were nevertheless, as usual, genuine, sincere and born of respect.

It certainly did not even dawn on me that the prophet was, in this instance, out of order, ungrateful, misdirected, human, wrong. Instead, I thought, 'If the prophet is angry with me, then I must be wrong.'

A Levite singer had decided to break away from the band, contrary to the ruling of the prophet. Going contrary to the prophet's dictates was something rarely done, but the Levite insisted on this career move. The prophet was angry, I knew, and contemplated barring him from performing in functions within the house – a humiliating and deflating fate. I had the prophet's ear at the time, and appealed on his behalf.

Some time after, I was going to visit my sister in the country. The prophet and this Levite happened to be accompanying me, as chance would have it. My sister was not at home, so we were sitting outside passing the time until she arrived. To this day, I don't know what I said or did, certainly innocently, for I 'worshipped' the prophet, but the two ghetto-based men turned on me, jived and ridiculed me almost to tears. And when, to escape their tongue lashing, I excused myself to wash my car in the meanwhile, the whole story of it being but a machine resurfaced. How would I have known that they were both jealous of the fact that I had regular access to a car and this lovely home and they had none? I bore my hurt, customarily, silently. Such a naïve, foolish innocent had I become that thoughts of unkindness, ingratitude and envy on their part never even entered my mind. What did was guilt and shame for past sins.

Sister Naphtali was very poor, as stated before, and I sought to assist her however I could. She was a tribe elder, and I respected her as such, and, by my logic, a much senior spirit to me. This day in question I was down and out emotionally and visited the headquarters for fellowship. The kindest comment I received from her was, 'That Naphtali brethren doesn't look like he will make it', to laughter.

One of my principal ways to recognition within the house had to be cricket. I involved myself in this aspect of the house's operation with usual passion. Soon thereafter, on the death of the captain, the vice-captain was elevated to captain, and I was elected vice-captain. I later found out this had much to do with my access to a car. I was given responsibility for the gear and for ensuring that we procured the field for practice whenever we needed it. There were two fields available, and numerous teams vying for the use of each. I had to reach it first, plant our stumps in the ground, act fiercely and ensure that none of the other teams uprooted our stumps to plant theirs, thereby staking claim. Sometimes, other brethren came early enough to provide additional backup force, sometimes none other came, but somehow we managed to have a field when required, and the gear was always there. This day, however, rushing from the farm I forgot to pick up some of the gear I had left at home. All but one sympathetic brethren cursed me without mercy. I felt like a pariah. But how could I, even for this one time, have forgotten some of the gear and denied the brethren a full fledged practice?

There will be trials and tribulation to bear, no weak heart can enter, His Majesty's work must be done at all costs, why had I allowed myself to have sinned so? were all thoughts I travelled with.

We were early on the Hill, that same precarious hill. The rift between Judah and myself had existed but the ties of the long, close friendship had not yet been severed. To this day, I know not whether he 'set me up' or not. He placed his bag at a strange point, difficult to reach, and walked off. Shortly after, he asked me to pass it to him. Not knowing how to say no, I attempted, and in so doing slid down the hillside crashing

74

into the section reserved for women and children, damaging one of the already limited seats. I felt like a spectacular fool, speechless.

'Some of these brethren don't know to stand up like men,' said a sister. 'Some of these new ones just won't make it.'

Imagine the effect on introverted, shy me, a twenty-six-year-old man of past professional excellence. Once again I felt like a boy: punishment humiliating and humbling. Didn't I pay my penance where humility is concerned? And wasn't I the epitome of folly?

The house had been established a few years before I joined. A few uptowners had, before my time, become members. Prior to their joining, the house was exclusively a poor people's organisation. At my time of joining it was still predominantly so.

The 'old guards', now sensing an invasion by people of a different social background, resisted zealously and suspiciously any seeming attempt at control, though being quite receptive of any goodies we brought, even encouraging same as in the case of our music equipment, for which, incidentally, Ringo did not seek my permission to donate.

As managers of a successful band, now in the house, Ringo and I could justly claim a say in the music arm of the organisation, but the existing council fought this. Yet when they required clarification on aspects of the music trade, we were called on. Nevertheless, they guarded, probably understandably, their management positions from us.

Oh, how my fragile, introverted psyche was crushed in those early days, and I attributed it all to retributive punishment and/or trials and tribulation. Everybody took a kick at the over enthusiastic fool. The prophet took a few.

I remember seeing a most complete and desirable catalogue

representing almost all His Majesty said and did on his visit to Jamaica in 1966. The catalogue was in the possession of a band-member colleague, now turned member of the house as I had. This, to my mind, was definitely a collection the house should have at all cost – or, at least, a reproduction from it. I had by then had the prophet's ear to a small extent, unlike the owner of this gem. I hurried him into my car and drove him, with the catalogue, straight to Rastaman Heights into the presence of the prophet. The prophet was not impressed, and his insult to me came across as if he had said, 'You fool, it doesn't belong to me, so what's the big deal. Do you expect me to forcibly take it from him?' What I had expected was for him to appreciate the value of the catalogue and, as undisputed and respected head of the organisation, order the brethren, who would be willing and happy to comply, to have a copy produced, even with my assistance, for the house which usually displayed any available picture, saying or word of His Majesty, our King and God. Instead, the prophet burst my balloon and submerged my squib in water. Of course, to my mind the prophet could not act foolishly, even in an angry or upset state of mind, so therefore I was the stupid fool.

Nobody would believe this but it was true. On entering the House of Israel I realised that my education, commercial experience and status qualified me to set examples to this motley crew, and, in fact, I believed that this was one of the principal reasons why I was called. This was not indeed an unreasonable assumption, but as my consumption of herb grew, the picture, the practicality, the extent became clouded, skewed and exaggerated.

Each elder was permitted to hold an 'authorised' dance in his month as a personal fund raising function to his benefit. Dances by any other member in that period were taboo and would evoke the prophet's and the membership's wrath on and off the Hill.

The dances were, to me, lacking in some things though quite enjoyable. For one dance, Levi's, in June, I took to the country two men in a van and carried over enough bamboos, coconut boughs and banana strings to erect a very artistic booth from which I sold cane juice, mangoes, coconuts and coconut cakes. No one appreciated the planning, industry, creativity, enterprise and competence except me, as Levi was silently angry, some of the membership also and I suppose the prophet; though, in fairness to him, as a sign of goodwill he purchased one of my coconut cakes when he could safely have boycotted me as most did.

Somehow, without realising it, I just seemed to be going about things in the wrong way and now also, in hindsight, I must have been losing track of reality, for indeed I was now pretty close to the prophet and Levi himself was close enough for his wife to have given birth to his first son under my roof. Why then had I not discussed the matter with them before?

What hurt me a lot, especially in the early days, was when the untrained children of the brethren called me by my surname, untitled. It made me feel how much of a child I had become; child of God, yes, but not child of children. Where I was coming from, adults, even respectable ones, treated me with respect. Yet I hurt, silently, but still put a smile on my face as secretly I despised the attitude of their parents who should have reprimanded them. Only recently I realised what pleasure and pride it was to those parents to see their off-spring on equal footing with this man from uptown. Somehow, by divine design or not, I had just submerged myself in this movement ceasing to think my way through.

If you, accustomed to a better life, try to treat people of

poorer lifestyles in a manner designed to let them feel equal, they are going to go for that feeling of superiority and if this involves putting you down, they are going to do it time and time again; and if you accept the put-downs humbly they are going to do it yet more. Not all, but most of them behave in this manner. Unfortunately, I didn't know and must have been smoking too much herb to be realistic enough to discern what was happening. As a result I absorbed, innocently, numerous insults, seething inside but saying not a defensive word. Unmentionable trials, tribulation, punishment, I said to myself; and maybe they really were.

My wife and I had enjoyed an almost perfect marital relationship. On entering the House of Israel the quality of the relationship had deteriorated a bit until she had made the bold move to 'step up' and join me. Now, with my general deportment, unattractive deterioration in hygiene, constant herb smoking, negative change in how I spoke to and treated her, the embarrassing way in which I conducted my business projects, the indifference with which I approached our financial commitments, my arrogant conduct at home, and many more reasons, a crack was manifesting itself in the relationship as we disagreed and quarrelled frequently. Trials and tribulation, I said to myself, are part and parcel of the package. I refused to accept the fact that I had changed negatively and was a major part of the problem.

I had started my search for God and truth not having, in the remotest part of my imagination, the prospect that I would end up where I did, Rasta.

Coming from where I had, I knew not what to expect, but I was prepared to learn along the way, giving it my best shot.

I learnt early that these people, my brethren, were from a

different orientation and had attitudes and behavioural patterns dissimilar to any I had encountered in my life. If I was going to gain acceptance, I would have to earn it.

In time I had got reasonably close to the seat of power, the prophet, and realised, though not clearly enough at the time, that many resented my type enjoying any such closeness and tried how they could to shake us off. Being a shy, non-combative type, I was intimidated but hung in there resolutely. The snide remarks and constant 'screwface' of some made it clear that I, with my 'undreaded' hair and different social upbringing, was not considered by him or her as a brethren, and had no right to be so close to 'their' prophet, undreaded though he was too.

After Naphtali's dance, I was helping early in the morning to sweep up the premises to hand it back over to the lessors spotless. A group of my detractors were looking on, and informed me that, instead of sweeping up the place, I should be out there trying to borrow money from Babylon to hire a plane to take them back to Ethiopia; so if all I could do was sweep then I wasn't serving any purpose. I do agree there was a practical logic to the comment, except it didn't factor in that I had escaped the world of money and borrowing and was now simply not looking in that direction. Also there was masochistic comfort and expiation for me in the humble, unaccustomed act of sweeping. I didn't see many others doing likewise.

Many of the membership now accepted me with reasonably open, welcoming arms; many didn't, and I vowed that in time all were going to have to respect my commitment and my work within the organ. In the meantime I was simply going to absorb whatever was thrown at me.

I remember a few of us newer members journeying from

the country with one of those not-so-friendly-inclined-to-us
brethren riding in the car. He was telling of his long association with the organ, citing past experiences of and within the
house as we listened and questioned enthusiastically, intently
and trustfully. He slipped in some junk about the need to be
careful, when being beaten by the police or any other not to let
them beat you on the head – lest the head get burst and you
lose that spiritual contact with God, rendering on death your
soul never to reunite with God. He also told of the spiritual
terrors of the night that could creep upon an innocent,
unsuspecting new member and strangle him to death. I
listened fearfully, not sensible enough to realize that the
Danite brethren was merely trying to scare us off.

In time he, like many other previous detractors, grew to like
and respect me as a true brethren. I certainly worked my way
to acceptance by one and all, but wasn't around long enough
to enjoy the prize.

I did it by just being my kind, considerate, compassionate
self to one and all and their children.

I am not absolutely sure if it was the over ingestion of herb,
overdose of Bible study, the new surroundings, the lack of
money motivation, the guilt complex, culture shock, folly,
madness, act of God, act of the Devil or my true personality of
naïvety surfacing, but my efforts at business were, in hindsight, woefully silly, ill conceived and impractical.

Why didn't I, a man of proven professional competence,
figure out that all that efforts on the farm were not worth the
fuel I was expending to get there, not to mention the major
expenditure?

Why didn't I realise the simple fact that while I was
stockpiling coconuts, to capitalise on the scarcity, they would

spoil? Those I took back to the country to convert to coconut
oil never did guarantee enough returns to justify the expenditure and effort. Why hadn't I done some feasibility analysis?
And when I tried ripening my stocks of bananas, most
spoiled, creating on top of other problems one of waste
disposal.

I rented an old grinding mill in one part of the country,
transported cane from my farm in another part, got cane juice
which I had to transport back to Kingston to seek uncertain
markets at schools and colleges, and ended up, as usual, with
the major portion spoilt. Having no real knowledge in wine
making, and being one disinclined to seek help, I sought to
convert some of the wastage into wine and failed miserably in
this regard also.

Matches, the prophet said, would soon be in short supply.
Wherever I saw them I purchased stocks for business and for
gifts to the brethren when the scarcity hit. I don't even know
what became of them.

I did not know how soon my time to go to Ethiopia would
come but I knew all kinds of seeds would be required for
planting. I never ate an orange or any other seed-bearing fruit
without storing the seed. Whatever became of those seeds?

A blood sister of mine enquired how she could help me and
offered aid to fix up my crashed VW. Uncharacteristically, I
borrowed money from two cousins who had always liked me.
I spent a little on the car, but not enough to get it going,
enjoyed some good servings of excellent herb, helped out
some brethren in trouble and invested in a stage show at
which the band would perform.

The venue was at a high school in the country and many of
the artistes from the house were contracted. Close to starting
time, there were probably ten paying patrons of the hundreds

I anticipated. I quietly slipped away to hide from the pressure in the adjoining headmaster's premises, to buy time until the place filled up some more. Sitting on one of the terraces, smoking my herb, for what seemed like hours, I observed from a distance a large animal like a dog or a lion or a cross between. I held my position, as he seemed to be approaching my direction, preferring to face this terror than the one back at the venue. I closed my eyes, tried to hold my breath and prayed as I heard the footsteps of the beast. After a while, I heard no footsteps and opened my eyes. Where the beast had gone I knew not, but shortly afterwards I went to face the music, calculating the various areas of hostilities awaiting me. My old band companions now on Ringo's side as opposed to mine, Ringo now overtly my adversary, the various artistes, the other non-paying brethren who had made the trip, the minibus owner, and also the van owner who had transported the instruments – all those I was sure would be hostile to me if enough people didn't turn up for the function. As it turned out, nothing close to enough had come. I promised part payment to all and they really were not all that hostile anyway, certainly not to the extent I had anticipated.

Having faced the music, I decided to listen and enjoy the offering and did just that. Eventually, some people got part payment, some did not, as my little stock of capital vanished again.

Trials, tribulation, punishment for true.

6

Joy Within

I had loved cricket as a boy, playing sometimes even at night and in rainfall along with my brothers and my friends. At high school and at college after, cricket was the most consuming and enjoyable aspect of my existence. The only time I was out of touch with cricket was a year when I was so frustrated that I had not, owing to many reasons, some fortuitous, fulfilled my dreams and aspirations of becoming a great cricketer.

Here, within the house, a second chance, which I had long given up hope of, presented itself, and with it the added motivation of playing on God's team of all the teams! It was as if I had been picked in heaven, from my birth, to represent the Almighty God at the sport of cricket. There was trepidation accompanied by fear and my usual doubts as to whether this time I would measure up to my full potential, but my joy was tremendous. I saw myself, also, functioning in the capacity of administrator, assisting my not so educated and exposed brethren to rise up to heights on and off the field, functioning in a manner exemplary and befitting representation of the King of Kings and Lord of Lords, our God. And what an encouraging thought, that of the glory of excelling in the presence of the membership, which attended each match in large numbers; then to be mentioned positively on the Hill, to walk tall and proud, winning acceptance from all strata within the organisation. Not initially, but eventually, I did win that type of status and enjoyed the trimmings that went with success, learning in the process that with yet more effort and sacrifice excellence could be maintained and greater success reaped and enjoyed.

Funny how little things can be pleasing and encouraging to the soul. One dread, a member, formerly a detractor, told me how he had braved it out of his volatile ghetto community to come to see me bat. On arriving at the match, and seeing that my innings had ended, he took the next bus back home. He should really have stayed and cheered on the team but his comment nonetheless made me feel good, very accomplished.

And as a bowler, my performance eventually made me feel worthy to bowl to the great Vivian Richards, the international batting superstar should such an unlikely opportunity present itself. And there was this sister who confided in me how much she looked forward to coming to see me bat, bowl and perform in the field. Eventually I was satisfied, fulfilled and happy with my game and my overall involvement in this aspect of the 'work'.

As vice-captain of the team, I became a member of the executive of the cricket fraternity, attending and hosting meetings to do with all aspects of the game's development within the house, including fund raising. All my previous training in the different spheres, though now tainted with a degree of impracticality, came in handy. And as I did my part commitedly, so was I accepted by many, within and without the cricket fraternity.

In my first year, my cricket performance was average, like the team's, but in the second year I was excellence itself, as was the team. We beat all comers in our league, and quite convincingly so.

The House of Israel cricket team trained hard almost every evening, ending each session with prayers and the Ethiopian anthem; then into brotherly reasoning and ingestion of good collie herb. I dearly enjoyed the camaraderie that had now developed, and when we met at celebrations, dances or any other function, we, the cricketers, hung together as one big family. I was as happy and fulfilled as at any time in my life then.

And when the other sporting groups had their activities, I was there, as also many other brethren and sisters, cheering them on and revelling in the fact that 'Israel' was so well represented on so many fronts. There were other groups too – music, drama, sewing, art, craft, dancing among others. I took a particular interest in the dancing troupe, having struck up a platonic relationship with a strikingly beautiful young sister, a member of the troupe, who kept me rejuvenated mentally and emotionally.

Within the house, there was something happening almost daily that was exciting and interesting. Even the paying of dues brought one in touch with many brethren and sisters, allowing for much reasoning and learning, and, of course, herb smoking. Yet again, one just had to visit Rastaman's Heights, where the prophet and many other members lived, to feel good. Apart from the much reasoning, interaction, sense of oneness, and herb, just being in the presence of the prophet was a great comfort and fulfilment. One felt like our brothers of old must have felt in the company of Moses, their conduit to God.

I enjoyed being kind to the less provided for, and would offer them lifts to their various destinations, though with a great degree of fear, for the very deportment of some, the obvious poverty, would certainly attract the police to me if encountered. Some of these brethren had so long ago withdrawn from society, barefooted even, that they bore no semblance to what society would consider remotely acceptable, and spoke a language foreign to English. So poor materially were some, I frankly don't think they had entered a motor car before. On helping them home I always experienced a sense of accomplishment and a feeling of pride that I did not take the easy way out: namely, that of filling the car with too many 'presentables' whose need was not as extreme.

I enjoyed the dances which were, legitimately, at least once a month. Nowhere in my life can I remember being touched emotionally as listening to the in-house sound system – Jehovah Music – especially in the wee hours of the morning. All those old standards that had touched something in me, as a child upward, were played, and in what seemed to be the perfect sequence and with the right balance of tones. Hit after hit just kept on coming in a soothing, relaxing, nostalgic vein, as music became ecstasy and continued ecstasy led to bliss. And when I thought I was pleasure saturated, the next selection took me yet joyfully higher. Mixed with the good herb, the potent roots wine, the camaraderie and love of those close brethren around me, I knew I had found heaven on earth, even if temporarily. Those were the happiest wee hours of my entire life, and when I focused on the DJ and he rode the rhythm like a lizard on a limb as inseparably as bone and marrow, injecting into the moment sweet, clear, appropriate musical reminders pertaining to our God and King, then I knew this was not only heaven but seventh heaven.

As I rocked coolly, reminisced widely, while focusing on the music, I said to myself, 'How good and pleasant it is to be a chosen of God.'

As I said before, there were trials and tribulation and punishment but there was also joy, great joy.

I had so passionately wanted the love, companionship and acceptance of my brethren and sisters and now, eventually, I had it to an extent and I was delighted. With the exception of a few, I was known, liked and respected, as far as I could perceive.

Who doesn't like music? I certainly do. In no prior association in my life was music more present. Every member of the organisation, almost, was a singer or player of music. As a result, music, Rasta reggae music, was everywhere, and I loved it. There was 'my' band, there was the original band of the organ, both of which I was exposed to at rehearsals, at the various celebrations, at stage shows. I was also exposed to the numerous artistes within the house.

At the functions, both bands played as the friendly yet real rivalry was evident to me, and this made the end product even better and more thrilling. Those within the house, accustomed by orientation to roots music, seemed to me to prefer the more refined sound of 'my' band. Some, like myself, accustomed to 'our' sound, preferred the roots sound of the original organ band.

The music, along with other facets of the existence, should have made me constantly happy. The only reason why I was not was that, somehow, I had forgotten that the pursuit of happiness was one of the principal functions of life. I had early, on entering the house, sought expiation through self-denial, much as one developed a death wish. I remember travelling with some brethren and sisters in my car. They

wanted to splurge a bit on niceties like peanuts and choco-
lates. I ate none, for that money could have been more
appropriately used to feed poorer brethren and sisters. I had
simply lost track of how life was conducted in reality. Or, as I
now suspect, I had lost track of reality from early in my
association in the movement.

Hadn't I thought myself undeserving of happiness, I, in
retrospect, see that, in spite of some negative situations,
almost constant happiness could have been found. I can
vividly remember the various celebrations, the dances, the
wine, camaraderie and herb, on days like His Majesty's
birthday, the equivalent of the Christians' Christmas. We
celebrated his coronation day also. The anniversary date of
the Organisation of African Unity was also celebrated by
us. Separate and apart from these functions, there was at
least one dance per month. At those dances, held by each
elder in the month representing his tribe, the entire membership would bedeck themselves in the fanciest of outfits in
the colours representative of their tribe. Sometimes too, a
function would be held, and, for a show of uniformed
militancy, all the membership would be required to dress
in, say, khaki. Where these predominantly poor people found
the money to measure up to the requirement I don't know,
but everyone made an effort not only to find the stipulated
attire, but also to be extremely sharply dressed in it. How
ironical, it now seems, my seeing the expenditure on niceties
on myself as a waste, whilst the poorest of us spent lavishly
to be properly attired for a celebration. But, believe me,
these people, predominantly poor as they were, were the
proudest set of people I have ever encountered in life. We
considered ourselves children of the Most High and were correspondingly proud. Similarly suspicious we were of out-

siders, and no less were we defiant of any authority outside of our ranks.

After the elders had accomplished their dances, some of the earlier members were allowed to hold theirs, each getting, similarly, the full backing of the membership. There were also the 'send off' dances which preceded the departure of a brethren repatriated to home, Ethiopia. It seemed a miracle to me how such basically poor people managed to find the funds to keep up with all this activity.

Every function approved by the house was always attended by a high percentage of the membership. Still, throughout the house we all knew that each one must help the other and so he/she who did not have enough felt no embarrassment to ask for help and he/she who could provide that help felt compelled to give it, and happily.

There was also the period when we took our music, married to our doctrine, to the streets, offering all and sundry a look at us in devotional meetings, prior to us going into our stage show featuring our two bands, a host of artistes plus the recognised sound system within the house. At different times, we rented movie houses, inclusive of the most prestigious, to hold these functions as the brethren and sisters, dressed to kill, proudly sapped up the thrill of showing 'Babylon' that we too had a proud social fibre.

Our calendar of entertainment activities was quite full and at times even I enjoyed myself to the full. As I said before, in hindsight it appears that I had enough to be happy, almost constantly, but restricted myself by too much in this regard. But I did really enjoy some of the functions to the maximum.

This function being held at a brethren's home was not a major one. The two bands along with some artistes were on show. As it turned out, the great Bob Marley, from the tribe of Joseph, was on the island and attended the celebration. He decided to perform for his brethren and sisters, and when he was finished, I certainly felt as if I could hold no more joy – until the prophet led us into the singing of theme songs; then I experienced that joy which knows no bounds. The theme songs, introduced sometimes at the end of meetings or celebrations, or whenever there was a gathering of spirited brethren and sisters, did really help to lift a spirit into bliss. As we sang together with one heart, I felt that comfortable feeling of being joined together, more than emotionally, with these other human beings, under the principle of all for one and one for all. These songs, in praise of our God, our people, our heritage, our motherland and all related, plus lyrics in defiance of Babylon and all oppressors, were sung so passionately, someone leading the lyrics, that some of us found ourselves at a point of frenzy, in my case unbelievable, given my degree of introversion. But then again, the good herb was there to assist me along, freeing me of inhibitions.

The theme songs did, in fact, help to bind us together and did also help to fill our hearts with joy and satisfaction, though temporary, in spite of whatever problems existed in and around our lives.

Boy, were the stage shows fulfilling! The two bands were always entertaining and some of the artistes, whom they accompanied, took us to sustained peaks of ecstasy. To see the efforts of even those brethren and sisters who fell below par in standard filled my heart and being with a feeling of beatitude, pleasingly touching even to tears. It was touching, to me, to see ordinary persons take on the mantle of entertainer, their nervousness and trepidation disappearing more and more from the time they took the microphone, and to see that look of apprehension transformed into smiling confidence as the audience responded positively to the words and music, created over time in the hope of one day being able to perform this, in praise of your God, before the brethren. I could so easily identify with that electric emotion existing on the stage, and we being of one heart found ourselves sharing in a real sense the source of bliss existing on the stage. Some of the songs were not so well constructed lyrically, grammatically, substantially; but that did not matter, as the effort was one hundred per cent, the melody sweet and catchy and the words related to His Majesty, good generally, the hope of triumph and victory: things we all related to and found joy in. The point is, even the lowest performances, professionally, lifted us, certainly me, to joy, whilst, later in the night, the real professionals just simply took your heart and played with it, lifting you to ecstasy, Utopia and beyond. The societal pressure, at the time, was so extreme that when situations like these turned up for you to give vent to your repressed and suppressed joy, ecstasy came easy. And when recognised top professional artistes took the mike to praise, in our way, our King and God whilst entertaining the membership, visiting brethren the elders and the prophet, ecstatic peaks kept rising higher and higher. I simply cannot find competence enough to describe the joy in my heart when the band played the introductory bars to 'Red Locks', 'Joy in my Heart' or 'Peace, Love and Harmony' or 'Live Good' or the 'King of Kings and Lord of Lords', to name a few; and of course there were others too who transported me to heaven almost to the degree 'Red Locks' did.

I have been through a lot since that time, yet the remembrance of the joy of those occasions does really linger, in a significant way, in the corridors of my heart, just as I can still picture the pride on the faces of the brethren and sisters performing then, at the various venues.

The delight I experienced within the house, at times, was not exclusively music related. I certainly did enjoy also those trips to the rural areas when the prophet decided to take the message of the House of Israel islandwide. As a young boy, I had so anticipated those rare excursions organised from the district, and when the day came closer and closer, my excitement elevated to frenzied proportions! The day after, I felt low and deflated, there being nothing to look forward to joyously in a long, long time.

These excursions, many years later, were anticipated with no less joy and with the added feature that, on returning from one, I knew that, within a month's time, there would be another until all fourteen parishes were duly visited by the house; and then some other missions would be created. I derived further happiness from the fact that all this was in the name of God, our God, the Creator, and on each excursion new recruits would be taken on board.

The outing to a different parish each month provided for myself and certainly most others a welcome change of venue, a new atmosphere, new experiences and, among other things, new types and quality of herb to taste and enjoy.

The unity and closeness created amongst the membership as a result of these journeys together, was to me strengthening, encouraging and warmth-inspiring.

I must confess I experienced always a feeling of great pride and satisfaction when the attire of the elders, the order, the discipline, the entire proceeding evoked a new respect for Rasta, a statement usually confirmed by the long lines of those wishing to step up. There was, of course, joy also in the simple fact that the movement was expanding numerically and tied to this fact was greater strength in all regards inclusive of physical protection and security.

To be quite frank, I derived quite some satisfaction in being able to show off to others, less enlightened in this regard, that which I was a part of and proud of.

Additionally, the sharing, the caring, the brotherly love emanating spontaneously as we journeyed together, as of old, filled my sentimental heart with such deep feelings of love, joy and gratitude to be chosen to be a part of such moments.

My sojourn in the House of Israel was certainly not all joy and bliss. In fact some experiences were the worst of my life. It is a fact, however, that there was some joy within. How many have experienced the sense of security in knowing God and knowing that he knew you? That, my friend, is a taste of comfort and safety, and these emotions represented the foundation on which further joy was accommodated and trials, tribulation or punishment prevented from causing permanent hurt. With these feelings, death no longer evoked so great a terror, for eternal life now had real meaning. Faith too, in the circumstances, almost became tangibly touchable by its realness, its lived reality. Whatever the difficulties, and they were myriad, there was this omnipotent, omniscient authority to call on, not as Babylon did, but as a God to whom we could relate, having lived amongst us humans in this dispensation, Christ in His Kingly character, the God of Israel, His Majesty.

While I was growing up, courage was never a strong point of mine, yet God had called me to duty and I had found the courage to respond positively. This was a source of pride and joy to me and any time I overcame any other hurdle in those days I experienced similar pride and joy.

Such comfort and satisfaction I derived from the knowledge that my God and King was none other than His Imperial

Majesty, King of Kings, Lord of Lords, Conquering Lion of the Tribe of Judah, elect of God, light of the world, earth's rightful ruler, Emmanuel – God with us; and He had indeed provided for us, His chosen, land in Ethiopia for us to return to, in time. He was our comforter and we felt comforted in this and enjoyed the related rapture. Whatever others said of Him, derogatorily, we knew to be Babylonian propaganda, designed with devious motives. We knew Him, felt Him undoubtedly in our lives, heard Him in our minds, understood Him, loved Him and gained much delight from all this.

But then again, it was common knowledge that the Almighty God had sent his Only Begotten Son to suffer on the cross to atone for our sins, epitomising the forgiving nature of God. Somehow I just never inclined my thought in that direction at the time. I suppose it sounded too much like the doctrine I was accustomed to prior to my involvement in the Twelve Tribes. Within this movement Jesus was known, recognised and respected by most, but only in so far as he had returned in the person of His Imperial Majesty Haile Selassie I. So forgiveness, a distant concept not applicable to me, I submerged my guilt-ridden self into punitive religious work via the organ, Twelve Tribes. The concept of forgiveness absent, every unpleasant experience that visited me, I attributed to punishment, relative to my dubious past. Some though, I accepted as the normal trials and tribulations associated with my becoming a Rastafarian, a disciple of His Imperial Majesty, Haile Selassie I, King of Kings, Lord of Lords, conquering Lion of the Tribe of Judah, our God.

7

Places

As a Rastaman, my lifestyle had been completely transformed, so revolutionised that I now wonder if, without the intoxication of herb, I could have dealt with it. I was accustomed to get up in the morning, prepare myself and head for work well and appropriately dressed, being treated at work in a manner consistent with that accorded a top, if not *the* top, producer, in a leading real estate brokerage company, nationally. Throughout the working day I would rub shoulders with and advise wealthy, powerful persons, those upwardly mobile heading for success, and myriad others. At the end of the day I might be at a client's home, a club or a hotel having drinks whilst doing business. Back at home, my wife and I would probably be preparing to attend a function, visit friends or relatives or be heading out for a meal or drinks. And, of course, I would find time to attend band rehearsals and be there at every engagement at the various venues, posh and otherwise, all over the island. Throughout the day my appointments would take me from site to site, from office to office, situation to situation – all in search of material success and social well-being, as was the norm.

In my conversion to Rasta, all that changed most dramatically. The transition is best analogised by a comparison of leaving uptown and not simply going downtown, but underground – underground not in the sense of criminal activities but in terms of visibility socially, religiously, materially.

When I married I had prudently and frugally decided to accept my wife's suggestion for us to rent, at peppercorn, a home owned by her parents in a modest lower-middle neighbourhood. After a few months, I decided to purchase a lovely and spacious three bedroom townhouse in a middle-class development. The unit I had selected was next door to the one I had earlier sold to a longstanding friend of mine. My wife had seen to the furnishing of the home, had covered the courtyard to the back and installed a hammock there for my additional comfort and relaxation. The helper's room was vacant at the time, the second bedroom was the guest room and the third she arranged with the necessary shelves et cetera for my library cum study. On conversion, I transformed this room into 'His Majesty's room' and filled it with everything I could get my hand on pertaining to my God and King. This room now became my point of worship, prayer, religious study, meditation as well as work, and I spent quantity and quality time therein. In this room also I smoked 'ton loads' of herb, sometimes in the company of others, mostly brethren. Physically, outside of transforming the third bedroom there were no great changes at the outset of conversion, though shortly after I started to use the courtyard and parts of the massive kitchen to store coconuts and related produce and cane juice. The majority of changes were not physical, but social. This neighbourhood contained exclusively upwardly mobile professionals. The very thought of a Rasta residing there was repulsive if not vomit-evoking, and for the smell of herb to be constantly in the air, and, of all things, for ghetto-looking dreadlocks Rastas to be passing through, must have been extremely upsetting to my neighbours. And to add to this I soon started falling down on my maintenance payments and thereby contributing to the deterioration in respect of the upkeep of the common areas, swimming pool and all. In time also, the cosmetic appearance of my unit deteriorated, especially inside, as my wife was left with the sole burden of carrying on financially; the mortgage payments had earlier started to lag behind.

But here at home was my safety zone. On the road, the police stopped me almost daily, searching for anything, especially herb, on which to base incarceration. I had my stock well hidden in my jockstraps and, if I were smoking whilst driving, I would have gotten rid of the spliff before being confronted by the police. The usual search of my person, while other vehicles passed by, the occupants of which sometimes recognised me, was humiliating, to say the least; embarrassing especially early after conversion, especially for a man accustomed to a different stature and consequent treatment.

No police, at the time, would seek to search my home, located where it was, but at any rate, being quite careful and afraid, I had my stock so well hidden I sometimes had a little difficulty finding it myself. At my residence I was safe, the socio-economic status insulating me against the harassment I encountered away from home.

My good friend next door, Immanuel, must have wondered what the hell was happening to me, none knowing how to approach me on the sensitive issue, but he must have wondered at the constant herb smoking, the constant influx of Rasta, the unusual shabbiness of my attire, the obvious drop out from society in terms of material pursuit and otherwise. I, of all persons, he must have thought, one previously so upwardly mobile and successful. He must also have been concerned, like others in the community, about the negative effect I was likely to create on their real estate values. Strangely enough, these considerations never entered my mind then, just like my own material welfare, precarious as it grew to become, never troubled my mind enough then.

Immanuel and myself, nonetheless, still maintained a close enough relationship although our goals and commitment and pursuits were so different. I adored his children and often conversed with them. We also played dominoes and Scrabble together but, in fact, the real friendship originating from college days was gone, replaced by mere cordiality, the gap between Rasta and upwardly mobile being too large, at that time, for friendship to span. My other friendships, even closer ones, had simply disintegrated. Probably if they were living next door also, strong enough threads would have existed to span the cordiality gap. Still I understood that, like myself, not knowing if I was still welcome to their friendship, they were probably faced with the same predicament. One of the few who visited more than once was my dentist, my cousin, but I was so high on my new religion, herb and anger against Babylon, I might have pushed away that hand of friendship, as I became more and more arrogant, unsociable and intolerant of the children of Babylon.

When my wife joined me as a member of the house, my home became more opened up to members. Very few of these abjectly poor brothers and sisters had ever visited in such a neighbourhood, unless probably working as a maid or gardener, so the opportunity to stop by was tempting to many.

They would be guaranteed unaccustomed comfort, some food, herb freely smoked and an opportunity to feel more important than their usual status allowed. To my mind, this was why God gave me the privilege of custodianship of this house, because he knew I would share it. The situation also presented me the opportunity of getting close to members, thereby gaining quick acceptability and respect towards becoming a recognised member of the organisation. Why it was so important and necessary for me to be outstanding I am just now understanding.

My wife was essentially the same young woman I had married, the home had not significantly changed. I don't suppose anybody or anything had changed so significantly except my outlook. In hindsight, I realise that I was so absolutely intoxicated on so many fronts I had lost my real personality. I was over intoxicated on herb for sure, Bible most likely, the doctrine of Rastafari most definitely. So lost was I, I was neglecting even the beautiful young woman I had so loved and married. I had forgotten that life was about pleasure and happiness instead of exclusive devotion to God.

Within two years of membership in the House, my prayers were answered and my daughter was born. She added a deep dimension of love and family to my life, though being so grateful to God for this bundle of joy meant to me payment or show of appreciation to Him in terms of more passionate commitment to the cause.

My residence now was home to my wife, daughter, her nanny and myself; but it was also home to many others temporarily, the lowliest within the house to the prophet, in time.

Pigeon Hill is where my 'farm', if you could call it a farm, was located. More precisely this was where the lands I decided to farm were located.

A couple of years before, Ringo and I, meeting with tremendous success at real estate sales, had branched out into real estate ownership. We had earlier bought, jointly, three residential lots and now sought to acquire this fifty-acre holding from a guy who, as it turned out, had entered in an arrangement to purchase from a guy who had entered in an arrangement to purchase from a rich landowner, subdividing for sale a vast acreage of which this holding formed a part. No title had yet been issued for this parcel; but, in time, we anticipated, that aspect would be dealt with.

The fifty acres comprised two parcels, the smaller containing five acres fronting on a minor road, level in most parts except for where a beaten track led you uphill, past the spring where the district got its water, to the plateau where most of that parcel of land was located. The neighbours said the spring was not on our land. The diagram said it was. A little above the spring, on the plateau, we built a modest hut around the time I attempted to farm that plot.

From this plateau, there is a fairly treacherous track leading over a hill which linked this parcel with the remaining larger acreage. I figured Ringo, in whom I had so much confidence, would find a way to get the proposed road leading from the main road to the south, coming down the hill and connecting with the smaller parcel, to the north-east.

When we had agreed to purchase, we had no immediate plans for usage of the land, but now that we had embraced the Rastafarian faith and given up real estate sales, we had sought and gained authorisation to process the land from the registered proprietor.

On the larger tract lay five separate hills, from each of which a grand view of city and harbour was visible. There were also large level areas lending themselves, even begging, for agricultural development. There were areas too, especially to the rear northern boundary, where squatters had established agricultural fields of various crops. To the front, southern section, our proposed road, in accordance with the diagrammed right of way, would pass by the holdings of existing settlers. On my eastern side, there were a few settlers too, and to the western boundaries there were quite a few machete-wielding squatters. The machete-wielding natives I discovered when the surveyor and I, in the company of others, sought to establish the boundaries of the entire holding. The settlers/squatters simply refused to let us complete survey of that section, brandishing their machetes defiantly.

Tests had proven the soil good for most crops, Ringo and I dreamt of establishing a family commune for brethren and ourselves; the first choice of hill for a house site would be the prophet's, the next choice I would offer Ringo and then I would choose from those left. This would be one model community, I mused, as I pulled on my spliff underneath one of the cooling trees. Strangely enough, the question of how the transformation would actually be effected never crossed my intoxicated mind.

We hired from the area three men, who got from our woodlands the necessary lumber which, combined with the zinc, nails etc. which we had brought in, quickly completed the shed, our farm house. They would continue to cut and carry fence posts to the hut where I counted off and paid them per acceptable one. Whilst the surveyor and I identified the boundary lines, someone would leave an appropriate mark, the fence hole digger would shortly pass behind as also the man placing the posts in the holes. The installation process would continue even after the surveyor and I had left for the day. With the posts intact, the barbed wire would soon be strewn and the property secured in so far as was possible. Either it was not to be, or I could not make it happen, but even before the machete wielders stopped us, threatening to chop up our rass claat if we proceeded further, the fence posts laid to that point were simply pulled out and stolen; many, I figured, ended up back on the heap to be paid for as new ones.

I decided to concentrate now on my five-acre plot, fenced with barbed wire, stupidly fencing in the spring. By the next day the fence was all down.

I was born the son of a farmer and whether because of high school away from home or not, I knew not enough of the occupation. Still, my parents had seen it unnecessary for me to learn much in this area, wanting for me a more progressive and prosperous future. The point is, now at age twenty-six, I, having already resigned my sales job, had embarked on the task of farming this five-acre plot myself, knowing much about real estate sales but very little about farming. As with everything I did at the time, I approached the matter with total passion, too much passion probably. I inherited the lands with some cane and planted more. I planted twelve different fruit trees as suggested by the prophet. I also planted pumpkin, yam, tomatoes, cabbage, onions, lettuce, carrots among other things and apportioned space to them proportionate to the results of my survey mentioned earlier.

I left from Kingston to my farm every day and can now remember the feeling of closeness to God evoked as my hands and body worked the soil. The earth is the Lord's and the fullness thereof, I told myself. I can remember, too, the feeling of accomplishment, fulfilment when, after a hard day's work I used the spring water to bathe myself; clothes changed, and refreshed, I enjoyed a spliff then set off for Kingston feeling like original man. Occasionally, I would leave directly from farm to a 'house' function or a dance. Those times I felt like a child of God, a prince of the tribe of Naphtali, travelling from his vineyard in the hills of Zion to attend to and or socialise with his brethren, children of the Almighty God, the God of creation.

The House of Israel had recently made the significant purchase of a brand new Mazda van. This caused quite some controversy; some unaccustomed to such a facility thought the purpose of this vehicle was to shuttle them here and there. Many times, on the Hill, the prophet had to reiterate that the Mazda was for 'official' business, meaning progressive missions. The farm, the prophet knew, would feed and house many brethren in time, so my venture was classified as official, and though my pride spurned the idea I was loaned the Mazda from time to time. One such time I used it to transport fertiliser and had a great quarrel with my workmen over the issue of fence posts. Ready to walk them out for effect, I couldn't find the key for the Mazda. Imagine me stuck in the remote hills with men I have just cursed off, and of all things, with the organ's Mazda which was no doubt required for other purposes, other official missions. Where in all this wooded acreage did I lose this damn key? Night enveloped us I started to panic until one of the men handed the key to me, his manner indicating that he had had many other options that were open to him concerning what to do with it.

Sometimes, members of the band, before we grew apart, journeyed with me to Pigeon Hill to give me assistance. Once,

I remember stopping for some beers at a bar at the nearest township, after work. Next door to the bar, a reasonable distance in from the road, was a small police station, officers from which were unlikely to have seen before four 'dreads' donned in their red, gold and green banners legitimately possessing a motorcar. I had not yet gone into the bar -- the others had -- when they approached, questioned and searched me. I remember one of my brethren coming out and stealthily reaching into the car and then disappearing swiftly. By the time the cops searched the car there was no herb to be found. My brethren had saved the day but had still retained enough to build two large spliffs. 'Close shave,' we agreed as we lighted up, now on our way.

Oh, what dreams I had for those fifty acres of land! A showpiece it would be, an example of the capabilities of God's chosen, the children of Israel. I would create a mini city of residences, vineyards, commercial and manufacturing ventures, totally Rastafarian in ownership and style. Probably my intoxicated insane mind was thinking five hundred acres instead of fifty.

Sometimes, not often, the prophet set out with me to visit the farm. During the journey to and fro, I asked him many questions on many things, accepting his answers as if coming straight from God. On the farm, we shared a couple of spliffs, discussed many topics, including the Scriptures, whilst inspecting my work on the farm, to date. I don't know that he knew much about farming in a practical sense, but his advice, criticisms and comments I accepted as from God Himself.

Ringo Judah, in respect of the farm, had concentrated mostly on opening up the bigger tract of the land by attempting to get roadways in. He had recently returned from a trip abroad, and came across to my side, criticising the manner in which I had planted out the crops. This he was doing, condescendingly, in a manner as if I were employed by him, and all this in front of those I had employed. I was hurt for many justified reasons, but most of all because I knew he thought that as Judah, I a Naphtalite was inferior to him. Here at Pigeon Hill, the rift between Ringo and myself widened. Ringo Judah even sought to chasten me for spending too much time on cricket. Who made him my custodian or my employer?

I was taking my involvement in cricket within the house most seriously and trained very hard. At Pigeon Hill, I would sprint all the way up the hilly track to the plateau; however, nothing contributed to my fitness like working the ground, weeding, forking, hoeing, planting, transplanting, reaping, etc. Apart from gaining fitness, working the soil filled me with much inspiration and motivation to go all the way for His Imperial Majesty, God, the Creator.

With a title for the land, loan financing was unlikely; without it, impossible. I nonetheless made efforts to avail myself of cheap government loan funds, under the Rural Land Development programme, but was unsuccessful. Benefits like these were not, at that time, available to the likes of Rasta, so my lovely proposal would have found approval for the rubbish bin. Still, in hindsight, that was a blessing in disguise, for indeed, the loan capital would quite possibly have ended up in the same bottomless pit my own equity did, the stinking fund.

I had previously excelled at sales and managed various valuable acquisitions. I did not fully understand all the intricacies of business, but had managed reasonably well before. Now, at that time, though they did not seem so to me, my business plans and approach bore no resemblance to practicality and seemed founded in unreality as I, more and more, leaned on the herb for wisdom and consultation.

Socially, life had turned so sharply for me; my lifestyle, the places I frequented, had so changed. When not at home, I was at Pigeon Hill, or Rastaman's Heights, at dues headquarters or a few other places all to do with Rasta.

Not everyone, but most residents were Rasta; not everyone but most of these were Twelve Tribes Rasta, certainly as far down on the road as I had ventured since I had known of its existence, and this only since the prophet had relocated here, having been forced out of the inner city ghetto by political activists. This was just around the time I had stepped up. I had heretofore had nothing to do directly with any ghetto; now I was a regular visitor to Rastaman's Heights. The entrance road off the main was a dirt track characterised by hills and valleys which, at some parts, had boulders protruding, occasioning careful manoeuvering of one's motor vehicle to avoid destruction of engine and undercarriage. The prophet lived a little way in, where another track led you up a short steep incline to a plateau which provided sites for his little shack and that of two other brethren, their families and his own family.

Obviously all residents of the area were very poor, but although turning off the main road I always experienced a bolt of fear, it was far less than that which had encompassed me visiting his previous place of residence which was most certainly a terrible ghetto community where warfare erupted regularly. Rastaman's Heights was different, and though the shacks were just that, there seemed more space, more green, more individuality, more peace. Of course there were illegal guns in this area too, but much fewer and less threatening.

Rastaman's Heights gave the feeling of being out of town though it really wasn't, strictly speaking, but in comparison to the inner city ghettos it could be considered so.

There were quite a few brethren around, some of whom had recently captured lands to relocate near to the prophet. I soon learnt that not all inhabitants were friendly to us Israelites, so militancy had to be maintained to ensure the prophet's protection at all times. For this reason, and many more, brethren and sisters were always present in numbers in the yard housing the prophet.

At the prophet's yard in Rastaman's Heights, we all passed through sitting, as it were, at the feet of Gamaliel, learning and reasoning one with another on doctrine, the Scriptures, life generally and everything pertaining to Jah, us his children and the House of Israel. Generally, the elders and more experienced brethren would impart knowledge to us newcomers, and he or she who managed to gain the prophet's ear would benefit from the most profound wisdom, knowledge and understanding, that he possessed. Many times, day and night, I would visit, managing sometimes to sit and reason with him in his house, on the bench outside, on the hillside or by his hammock set back a little from his house. Often we shared a spliff as I sought his advice on things, many of which I really should have thought out myself. We all depended on him too much, the elders not being considered and installed as the practical assistants they should have been in a structured order of command. Soon, being one of the few with a motorcar, I became one of his unofficial chauffeurs.

Rastaman's Heights was a significant though informal meeting place of the organ. From here I learnt, first hand, of the happenings in the various ghettos and communities in which the members lived, the gang wars, the political wars, police brutality, feuds between members, trials and tribulation of all sorts. And if an important message was to be sent to any member it simply had to he aired at the 'meeting place' and in no time it reached the desired destination however far. This we called 'sending a sound'.

When I had joined, the 'mystery frame' was kept at Rastaman's Heights. Photographs were always being taken by the prophet or on his instructions. Through a mysterious process which I still don't understand, certain of these were chosen and placed in a glass frame and hung conspicuously for the members to see. If your photograph managed to appear in the mystery frame you knew the eyes of the membership, the prophet and His Majesty were focusing on you, usually in a favourable way. I soon got into the frame a picture of me playing cricket. I felt sealed as a cricketing ambassador of the Most High, and of his people, Israel.

If a brethren was short of a meal or a draw of herb, a visit to this venue or any other meeting ground was likely to satisfy the need, as we all knew the responsibility to share. Many abused the privilege, I now know, seeking always.

Living in Rastaman's Heights, as I said, were many members; living close by were many more, including some paraplegic brethren, one of whom I sort of saw as part of my responsibility to assist financially.

There were other meeting places too.

The official headquarters, at the time I joined the organisation, was that place where we paid our weekly dues. It was, in fact, the home of two elders and their families, a first executive and a second executive.

I could afford to pay my dues weeks in advance, and so

did, but would still visit the headquarters almost weekly to see what enlightenment I could glean from the usually large gathering of brethren. I was my usual unsure, self-conscious, introverted self, but usually bolstered with herb, I made my way to headquarters to learn what I could, meet others, and know more and more of my brethren and pertinent matters.

I soon confirmed that the book in which the elders recorded the names of the members in respect of their dues was, in fact, the Lamb's Book of Life referred to in the Bible. So, indeed, when I had stepped up and presented myself at the headquarters with my passport-size pictures and dues to receive my dues book, at that time my name was indeed recorded in the Book of Life and I had therefore crossed the significant line from spiritual death into life eternal.

At the headquarters, like all other meeting places, the smell of herb was always present. Raids from the police, somehow, were not so frequent, and I always wondered why, as I kept nervously watching the entrance.

Still, I remembered hearing the reports of when the 'beasts' descended in their numbers. I was absent, many brethren and sisters weren't. The police harassed, brutalised, humiliated the brethren and sisters then carted them all off for incarceration. My heart filled with tears.

At the headquarters, I met again so many from early school days whose paths had not crossed with mine for so long, and they seemed always to be those whose spirits I had so admired and liked. I met also some superstars of music, sports, art, whose paths I never had thought would have crossed mine. Now they were my brothers, in love and unity.

One of the brethren, at whose home the headquarters was located, I remembered as one of the stars from my alma mater. He was now married to a beautiful sister highly educated like himself, both now comfortably resigned, along with their children, to the life of Israelites. Their sacrifice, in the work of God, it seemed to me, made mine pale by comparison.

Everywhere were dreadlocks, plus those dread in heart though not yet in hair, some friendly, some not so friendly, some with a permanent screwface.

Without your red, gold and green banner also, you could not enter the Hill; so, having ordered mine from a Zebulanite sister, I had picked it up from headquarters, one of the meeting places of the Twelve Tribes of Israel.

Before conversion, I was often with Ringo. In this regard nothing had changed much, except that I became more dependent on him for guidance until, of course, we had our falling out. Our paths still crossed often enough, but we now seldom visited each other. One of the fellows from the band married into my wife's family, and being someone I had quite liked he came by me sometimes, even giving me a day or two's labour at Pigeon Hill; sometimes I visited him. There were others too with whom I exchanged visits.

There was a brethren who controlled a big yard in a low-income area reasonably close to Rastaman's Heights. Many brethren, including myself, visited his place very often to soak up his relaxing ambience, eat one of the lovely meals he sold cheaply, or to sip of his roots juices. Of course, like everywhere we frequented, good herb was easily accessible, and the atmosphere lent itself to burning a few spliffs whilst involving ourselves in some good reasoning. Others too, following as opposed to members frequented this scene in search of reasoning, prior to making the bold move of stepping up.

This location was in walking distance of where cricket practices were held, and just as close to where the band rehearsals were done and as such was frequented by me. Of course, once a month, religiously, I made my journey to the Hill for meetings, and if there were public meetings elsewhere, I would be there.

There was one other location I visited often enough. I was twenty-six, she was nineteen, fresh, beautiful, bright, enthusiastic and comforting. This sister made me feel rejuvenated, important, knowledgeable, likeable; yet not once did we jump the moral fence into sexual activity. I was that lost to God.

Some aspects of my early upbringing caused me to be overawed by people. Some, I now realise, were less accomplished than I, yet, probably because of the confidence and assurance they emanated, I saw them as better than me. Even when I was at the point of success in my career, I had difficulty covertly holding to the belief that I was better at what I did than the others. The other guy, to my mind, just seemed more competent. As I had progressed in my chosen field, this psychological chip on my shoulder kept reducing. However, I entered the house of Israel with the misconception that all those who had found their way in before I had, were, irrespective of where they originated from, senior spirits to me and the executives were the equivalent of the management I had previously related to in the outside world. The prophet, of course, was the supreme unquestionable boss of the entire outfit. Whether this erroneous premise originated from the chip on my shoulder or the distorted perception created by marijuana use, I am not certain. I suspect a combination of both led to me being sidetracked by incorrect premises. Later in life, I was diagnosed as a manic depressive,

so it was quite likely that from the beginning of my relationship with Israel, from the time I started smoking the weed, I
had started my trek to insanity, as later manic depressive
episodes verified.

8

Persons Within /
The Members

How does one describe Ringo? Firstly I must say he was a big influence in my life. Were it not for him, I don't think I would have gone the Rasta route. And even before that, he had helped me become a more productive, noteworthy sales achiever. Although I had introduced him into real estate sales and exposed him to my experience in the field, in honesty it was he who pulled me out of my shell enough to come close to my full potential as a producer. His pull too made me accept the offer to get involved with the management of the band. All told, he was probably too great an influence.

He was from a country town where his parents were prominent citizens, and although in matters academic he didn't excel, he exuded the confidence of one proud of his station in life ... and was he an extrovert! Extroverts tend to be likeable to many, disliked by some who interpret aspects of their personality as boastfulness. I don't, however, remember many disliking him, other than a few who I thought were jealous of him for his apparent mastery over life, and certainly its causes for inhibition.

In the early stages I, like many, found him a live wire, likeable, personable, kind, jovial and many such characteristics associated with a good, pleasant person, though possibly a little too effervescent.

I was then the chronic introvert, but disciplined, sober and perfection-inclined, so together we made a formidable combination in business, with him dynamiting, awakening and unearthing whilst I collected, cleaned up, stored and then displayed. And in revelry and other social aspects we got along just fine too. He was that friend who was closer than a brother, a key spar; but strangely enough, only until we entered the House of Israel.

To date, I can't fully comprehend how we became so apart. I know the excess of herb had altered both our personalities. I know some ties like the real estate and band relationship were no longer there. I strongly suspect, also, that I had found myself, and a new focus for hero worship, the prophet, whom we were both trying to impress somewhat rivalrously, at the time. Then, I had written off our broken ties as an Act of God, divine manipulations; but it never ceased to concern me that, in the House of God, instead of cementing closer unity we were at loggerheads.

Ringo, the popular 'with it' guy, would and did precede me in exposure to herb smoking, other roots pursuits and general search to what we then called 'being conscious'. I, not wanting to be classified as 'dealing with nothing', did soon follow suit. There were, however, other motivations which led me into my search for truth and consciousness.

Prior to conversion to Israel, I don't seem to remember in Ringo, or myself, any current inclination to religion, other than visiting church, occasionally. Did he, afterwards, however, devour the pages of the Bible, as I later did! I can remember the excitement, enthusiasm, fanaticism as he unearthed things in the Bible, showing me and the band boys the truths that had been hidden from us. As his eyes reddened further with herb, his voice became louder with religious fervour and passion as he explained to us the doctrine of the Twelve Tribes of Israel validated by the Holy Bible.

As we grew further apart, the other members of the group, the fellows from the band, inclined to his side. In many ways, I had held the team together, but I was more perceived as being the deputy and he, Ringo, the leader. I suppose that had he not, in my eyes, assumed the role of Judah and relegated me lower on the rung of respect, I would have continued to be happy in the role of deputy that I had grown accustomed to.

So we went our separate ways within the house, he gaining the respect of many, I likewise.

If my involvement in, experience of and from the Twelve Tribes sacrificial experience proves beneficial to my life, and that of others through me, then Ringo is worthy of a salute. If the converse is true, he still won't encounter blame from me, for he sought to introduce me to God, as he saw it, and I went in with eyes quite opened, though with herb.

I gave my all to the house when I was an active member, but no more than he did. He, in fact, managed to help the development and advancement of the movement most significantly in a few key areas.

Yea, before conversion, Ringo was one impressive character, judging by Babylonian standards. Upwardly mobile, he was with the sky as the limit; a brilliant and uninhibited salesman, always confident and self-assured, easy to communicate with, fearless, greedy for success and guaranteed it.

Physically, women obviously found him attractive and this included some pretty desirable ones. He was always dapperly, trend-settingly dressed, and I found him a hard act to follow in this regard. His cars were always late model trendy ones, and he managed somehow to make the interior as also the exterior so well maintained and attractive. And you could count on his taped selection of music to be 'what's happening' in music. I could see how an ordinary woman, as well as others not so ordinary, even the very desirable, were unlikely to leave his car not a little intoxicated. And of course, having picked her up, he knew exactly where to take her for excitement and entertainment. To my country boy's eyes he was a class act. It is not that I did not try to measure up to his standard, but I must confess, he bettered me.

I can remember many nights, after midnight, Ringo would awaken me to journey to a club or some activity spot, sales kit in hand, to tackle some wealthy acquaintances of his whilst they were in a good mood and a bit 'juiced' up. We closed many sales from junkets like these. In different strange circumstances too, we had contracts signed, sometimes with flashlight, car light, street lamp providing the lighting. He was a hard worker, fully charged enthusiastically, extremely motivated and absolutely dynamic, and his results in respect of sales closed and those he assisted confirms the truth of the statement.

In terms of the relationship with the band, most times he proffered to them solid, forward thinking advice, which they didn't take seriously enough at the time. I can just, even now, picture him showing the lead singer how to project himself, his being, his message, and how, with the use of his hands, to caress and control the audience from a distance.

The organisation had a way of dwarfing you whoever you were before, and wherever you were from. You knew you were now in God's House and, as such, a mere mortal not yet proven useful, in spite of your past accomplishments.

I saw Ringo Judah go through the dwarfing process much as I did, as we all seemed to start life and education all over in Kindergarten I. We were now, for the first time in years, not working together as a team, not compensating for each other's inadequacies and excesses, but instead closer to being enemies than friends.

Ringo and I had been inseparably close as friends and business partners. With all his blinding brilliance, it was I who had kept our boat afloat, Ringo being a complete stranger to details. It was I who controlled the purse strings to ensure that our families were fed, mine too, and that enough was invested feasibly and we each enjoyed enough comforts. Despite his brilliant performances, it was I who managed to bring in more income, whilst tying up Ringo's loose ends. We had also managed to touch a point of maturity where share of money relative to who earned it was unimportant. We had, in fact, passed the point in friendship where money had the power to come between us. For my part, I gave him the better of whatever we bought, cars, music sets, briefcases, whatever. Whether this was out of folly, decency, admiration or whatever, I simply don't know. And when he took off for a year to 'search', his monthly cheques never ceased. I found how he dealt with me in the organ too inconsistent with what had existed before, to the extent that I realised my hero worship was misplaced.

When I first met the prophet at his inner city abode, just prior to his moving to Rastaman's Heights, I was frankly unimpressed.

His short, rotund, pot-bellied frame and missing tooth presented a picture far removed from that which I had grown
accustomed to associating with knowledge and authority.
And when he spoke, I had difficulty making sense of what he
was saying, primarily as a result of his inarticulate English, in
respect of propriety of grammar, vocabulary and general
construction. I couldn't but wonder, my prejudice influencing
me, 'Why the hell is Ringo so convinced that this man, neither
locksed nor unlocksed, has all the answers to truth and life?'
Still I had been reading my Bible seriously, and it spoke
volumes of the children of Israel, a fact I noted. Ringo and
others were telling me that I was one, a chosen of God, an
Israelite, in this dispensation, come to set up the righteous
government of God. Of this I had also read in the Scriptures.
This unimpressive man, Ringo and others, had informed me,
held the key to all this. I was simply going to hang around, I
decided, decipher what he was saying, search it through and
see if sense indeed did lie therein.

In him, Ringo had found a hero, his leader, his counsellor,
his mentor, adviser and prophet. So he invited him to the
band engagements, and everywhere else, as honoured guest,
foisting him on all, unmindful of sensitivities and sensibilities.
With exposure, more and more, to him, I learnt to understand what he was saying and had really to admit that he
had overcome lack of formal training and found a way to
converse, confidently, with anyone. In time, I had to admit
to myself his tremendously wide knowledge, biblical and
otherwise, and more impressive it seemed in the light of
my having given up on other traditional authorities, experiencing now, for my own self, the true nature of the system
of which I had been a part. I found him to be, more and more,
a man of tremendous wisdom and understanding also, so

much like the seers, the prophets I had read of in the Good Book.

I came to accept him as the prophet of this time and the person to whose coat tail I would cling for spiritual and other leadership, the bank in which I would invest my future, the successor to the prophet Marcus Garvey, indeed.

As I grew to know him more and more, my love and respect for him grew to the extent that his well being and safety were real concerns of mine. He seemed genuinely just and fair, compassionate yet tough, fun loving yet disciplined and committed to order. Humanly fearful, yet courageously, fearlessly, passionately in love with and committed to God, he was understanding of our frailties, possessive of an anger, yet basically a peaceful man.

There was something mysterious, almost unearthly about his eyes that indicated a superiority of person, now visible to me, in spite of his innocuous bearing. He commanded love, respect, admiration, trust from the membership, except the recalcitrant few. And this respect did seem justified, for indeed, he had given us a new and desirable concept of self, moulded us together into an all for one, one for all unit, each prepared to spurn even family for this mission. Some of those who had been bent to this order and discipline were indeed of the fiercest and most ferocious looking individuals one could ever encounter. And they were now humbly, religiously, studying the Bible, whilst even, in time, relating to the likes of me as a brethren. I don't know if any can rule with a compassionate iron hand, but he came close.

He was a poor man but very proud, self-controlled enough though to take a few on the chin, without retaliation, from the powerful Babylonians' system. He seemed an honest man, but practical enough to seek a favourable opportunity to improve his lot, even in the light of some criticism.

The prophet, I found, had a propensity to speak in a parable-like manner which gave listeners different, even opposite interpretations. If you made a mistake as a result of your interpretation, he would quickly and vehemently deny having given that instruction. I frankly did not like this aspect, but at the time interpreted it as a necessary survival tactic, and at any rate who got fooled was probably to have so been. Later, wiser, I found the habit, more particularly the denial aspect, quite disturbing. Later too, no longer spellbound, I discerned contradiction in some of the things he said. Later still, with more objectivity of focus, I realised that like us all he had his failings. Once his authority, his dictatorship was challenged, the challenger was thrown to the wolves. But then again, similarly, to an extent, would such a usurper have been dealt with in the Old Testament, in Moses' or other prophets' time? This was a survivor of no mean order.

Was he a prophet of God? Now that I can see clearly, my eyes no longer too opened with herb, of a truth, for a man of very humble background he has accomplished much, very much; numerous branches worldwide are one of the attesters to this but so have other people done. How did he impact on my life spiritually? Positively, is the truth. The next question in relation to the first is, were these Israelites raised up by him the true authentic people of God? If they are, then I must ascribe to him prophet status. Are they? The truth is, I still don't know for sure. I have no doubt that God can, in any dispensation, raise up a people especial to him and place within them similar spirits to that of his original chosen people, Israel. That is not difficult for me to take in, for it's a small thing for God to bring dry bones back to life and make of them a mighty people. And the location of this resurrection could as easily be Jamaica as any other country. Indeed, and in fact, Jamaica seems so blest with worldbeaters in every sphere, it absolutely defies probability.

There is no doubt in my mind that the membership was constituted to a large extent of very proud, committed, fearless, God fearing people, much unlike I had experienced anywhere else, and that great warmth, peace and love abided within the community. But was 'Jim Jones' cult any different, or for that matter 'Heaven's Gate' or like movement?

Looking now from the outside, I see to a great extent that there were also many (including some of the leadership) whose motives and actions were highly questionable.

Maybe the intention of the Almighty was to awaken the consciousness of the members, then some would go their way, enlightened to educate and instruct others religiously. Who was to remain within the house would so do. For myself, I learnt a lot within the house of Israel, enough to help guide others towards God. If I manage to accomplish certain things in my life, then Twelve Tribes would have been a positive contribution. In the meanwhile, I reserve my opinion as to whether they are the revived children of God, and their prophet a true one from God.

Of many matters related to my sojourn in the organ I have not yet formulated a conclusive position, but to be fair and just I must say that, despite normal human failings, the prophet did appear to be a good man with a mission, possessing the ability to predict future events, and having a manifest talent in organisation and control.

A great deal of the love, respect, admiration, hero worship showered on the prophet by me and others sprang from the fact that he was the leader, God's representative, the one who had opened our eyes and had rescued our lives from certain death unto life everlasting and as such was deserving of our gratitude. This is not to say he had not earned our love and respect as a result of his personality, character and performance, for he had. This is to say that Colin Lamb did not come with similar credentials but managed to win our love and admiration greatly, though nothing compared to that enjoyed by the prophet.

Colin was a strapping specimen of a man with a heart of gold, a commitment to duty and a sense of brotherly love and concern, to a degree emulatable even by someone like me, not short of similar attributes and type of character. He, on my entering the house, most epitomised my concept of brethren and established the standard that I desired to attain as a brethren.

He was soft spoken, but firm and uncompromising when it came to His Majesty's work, which dominated our entire lives.

When I mention my having to bail brethren, I could not, fairly mention it in the same vein as Colin's contribution in this area. Daily, and more often, he was at the police station dealing with freeing brethren from incarceration. Yet he found time to run his little furniture manufacturing business, in partnership, manage and control the cricket area within the house, and be of help in almost all aspects of the house's functioning. His old Chevrolet van was always filled beyond capacity, transporting brethren here, there and everywhere, including cricket practice. I can here remember him saying, of the Babylonians, whom he referred to as the uncircumcised, 'They are so unreliable they know not how to keep an appointment'. And, in truth, the degree of reliability and commitment to duty I encountered within the house made what I was coming from pale by comparison. I suppose, in fairness, this is something else the prophet should be commended for.

Colin was from the same country town as Ringo, and was of upbringing, socially and economically, not dissimilar to his. He had found his way into the house long before Ringo, and by the time I entered had earned a respectable position therein.

In whatever area of the house, from the dread, dread, dread screwfaces, to the newcomers like me, when Colin Lamb's name was mentioned it was with genuine respect, as a friend to all, a true brother.

Listing Colin's individual contributions defeats my memory, but to express the measure of my personal respect for the man, let me just say I can think of no one that impressed me so positively that I used him as my standard as to how I wanted to be remembered in terms of my interaction with my fellow man.

And aren't we all human? Like all Israelites, he loved to enjoy himself, and at the dances you could see the joy on his face as he swayed coolly to the sweet reggae sounds with a nice spliff in hand and a glass of original roots wine.

He was captain of the cricket team, and how he loved that sport and fought, against his absence of great talent, to perform creditably. I can now see the look on his face as the opposition had our backs against the wall: the look of purpose, commitment, concentration and prayer as he, our captain, marched out to save us; the fight, the struggle for mastery, as bat tackled ball and vice versa; eventually, the unrestrainable glitter in his eyes, brightening of the cheek and the bodily mannerisms reflective of his having succeeded at surpassing his best performance in his effort to save us from defeat; the increased loquacity, telling of the tensions that had had to be kept in check while the battle lasted; and the resultant relief now that it was over.

This is my last and most vivid recollection of my captain, my friend, my brother, mentor in part, as the next day Colin lost his life through drowning. God had taken Colin back. My heart bled with tears unshed, in public places. That Sunday's meeting was the saddest, most fearful I have ever attended, anywhere, any time, any place, any type of meeting.

I vowed to take up his mantle.

Adjudged as being from the tribe of Naphtali, I thought it the right and proper thing to get close to and assist, however possible, my tribe elders, male and female, and so did. My concentration, though, was on the first executives.

Brother Naphtali was a nice, humble individual with similar nervous energies to mine, and reminded me so much of my father, though less presentable socially by Babylonian standards.

He it was who had first responded positively to the prophet's call, stepped up sharing the early burden of the work. On entering the house and meeting him, as I got to know him, I recognised the great similarity of spirit that existed between us. He was gentle, meek, humble, self-conscious and filled with kind words, features I found typical of us Naphtalites. He was much older than I was and from a different background, but in time we grew closer and closer. I invited him to my home and also visited his in a ghetto area. In his neck of the residential jungle, I realised that with what I purchased a portion of herb for, close to my home, I got four times the quantity; so together, each time I visited, we consumed a few very large spliffs.

When he held his 'elders dance', shortly after I joined the organ, I made myself available to him, and at the end, did his accounting and was handed the proceeds for safekeeping. The thinking in the ghetto, the lifestyle dynamics were so different from what I would have been accustomed to.

When, for example, Brother Naphtali turned over the money to me, I wasn't even cognizant of the fact that any known source of money, lump sum especially, is an immediate focus of thieves in the area, and outside thieves even. And, of course, his home, like all the others there, was easy picking for burglars, unlike my well secured home. There were too many things I wasn't aware of, took for granted or simply did not think out.

After spotlessly cleaning up the premises we had rented, I reached home at daybreak, and shortly thereafter set out for Brother Naphtali's house, had a few spliffs while counting the money and doing the relevant accounts, then left for my home with the money entrusted to me. Tired, I slept until nighttime, went to my farm on awakening the next morning, thereafter visiting Brother Naphtali. He was trembling. The persons from whom he had borrowed capital, the workers, some suppliers had all passed through for their money. Additionally, the view was I must have made off with the money – which in their economy was a very large sum. Why didn't you contact my home? I asked him. The telephone is not a given in their existence and he had forgotten how to reach where I live, and at any rate even the cost of the bus fare was a relevant consideration. The time lag of one day had created a great dislocation within that scene of poverty. I simply did not know, having only recently touched this type of existence, that this was how things were down there.

During my stay in the organisation, I did have some interaction with Naphtali but, now I realise, not enough. Too much of my attention was centered on the top of the stream, the prophet.

Nothing was meek, humble and gentle about Sister Naphtali, I now realise, and I don't quite remember her for her kind and goodly words. She was of similar ilk, economically and socially, to Brother Naphtali, but where he never used his position as elder to solicit financial aid, she did; in fact she was too often seeking assistance. At the time, my mental blindness didn't allow me incisive vision enough to see her perception of me as a feeding tree instead of a brethren. I remember taking the prophet, herself and others, to a little party a brethren was holding. I had been away from home the entire day, and had used up my remaining cash in buying drinks and food for the group. As it turned out, she and I had to share a plate of food. By the time I turned my back, she had finished the meal and to tell the truth I was absolutely famished. I was very hungry, and would not reach home until late, so I was upset; but not to the extent of expressing it. As I reasoned to myself, she would not have known of my extreme hunger, or the fact that my money was finished, and at any rate, she knew food awaited me at home. I still thought that for her to consume all the food, knowing that it was for both of us, was damn selfish and thoughtless. There were many other comparable situations. On one occasion the house had travelled to distant Westmoreland as part of its round-the-island campaign. Returning the next morning, more than a thousand of us, the motorcade stopped at a most beautiful roadside beach for jollification. Poor people suffer a lot, so when they get a chance at enjoyment, especially of a different nature, they make the most of it. Now all of us got the very most of a situation when high on herb. Working, dancing, making love, whatever, we amplified the situation by having a spliff before, after or during, where possible. This brethren opened out his little cache of herb, poured it out in his spliff paper, flavoured it with a little tobacco from a half of cigarette. Rolling it carefully, lovingly, to perfection, he built his spliff with that look of joyful anticipation on his face, a look not far dissimilar to that associated with foreplay in anticipation of coitus. He started, with a car as shield, to undress prior to donning his swimming clothes. His friend came by begging, I surmised, a few draws of the carefully built spliff of significantly great size. His friend wandered away with the spliff. I turned my eyes away from the situation for a while. Minutes later, a verbal commotion beckoned back my attention as the wail of hurt, disappointment, frustration reminded me vaguely of a mother weeping for her child. The friend just could not have resisted the temptation to smoke most of it off.

Even if the victim had money enough to purchase another draw, which I doubt, where was he going to find anybody with enough to spare to sell at this time? Hardly was it possible that he would pass this lovely beach again in life and, trust me, he wasn't going to enjoy this swim that much without the intoxicating, inhibition-stilling state we had all discovered and loved. Many, most of us don't realise the deep-seated impact of things often referred to as little things. Little things mean a lot.

Somehow, I sort of had it all wrong. Just as I saw the elders as having perfectly pure and righteous spirits, similarly I credited the membership, especially those in before me, with seniority, and correspondingly treated them as such, to a great extent. Somehow, between over absorption of the Bible, Ringo's early tutoring, over intoxication on herb, general stupidity, culture shock, my lack of conventional friends, whatever else, I elevated my brethren to – and kept them at – a height where even their faults I perceived as something else.

When some new attractive sisters came on the Hill for the first time and this senior brethren Bongo Ray kept talking loudly after the order of 'One voice', I assumed that he had not heard that the meeting was about to begin. It never dawned on me that Ray was showing off to impress the sisters. Somehow, I thought that others, certainly seniors, would not do what I wouldn't because I shouldn't. When, for example, two brethren challenged each other to fight, I, like Moses, couldn't understand this; and when I left my farming implements in my unlocked car at cricket practice and found them missing, I knew it had to be an outsider, not a brethren. How could one be so naively trusting? On what visit had my reality gone? Still, there were numerous brethren who were solidly good, righteous, honest persons worthy of the pedestal on which I had placed them. And even those guilty of infractions were, for most part, basically good, caring, devoted, God conscious and God fearing people whose circumstances, financial and otherwise, made them fall prey to temptation more often than some of us. To see them in worship and service of their God, believe me, was something to behold; the sincerity was present.

Most of us brethren were what society referred to as lazy, worthless, malcontents, hooligans, more likely to disrupt and destroy than to build. Of a truth, many were resolved to do no more building of Babylon, looking to repatriation instead, so there was some basis for Babylon's dislike, and lack of respect. Yet when any brother or sister was called to duty within the house, the commitment to duty was total, whoever he/she may be, and to perform less than creditably was simply not accommodated. Working for Jah, Jehovah, God, The Almighty, His Imperial Majesty, all of us knew was a most serious responsibility. I had not seen the like or anything similar, even in party politics or business, certainly in terms of commitment. In any situation, you have a few who, for one reason or another, fall short. There were a few there too, but very few. And when you fell short and the 'sound' was circulated, or, worse yet, the matter was discussed on the Hill, you were worse than a pariah. Man, woman and child, your friends even, scorned, hurled insults at you, temporarily excommunicated you. Conversely, when you succeeded at your mission, you enjoyed superstar status for a long time. We all worked towards a taste of the latter. I have never, ever since, seen a group so collectively committed to duty in such an unflinchingly serious way.

Do, now, imagine what it felt like to accept the thought, convincingly, in your conscious and subconscious, that you were in lived reality a child of The Most High God, The Creator of the heavens and the earth. And he recognised you individually by name and tribe and you constantly heard his voice in your head, especially when 'high'. At all other times he was, in fact, but a prayer away, and the Scriptures you read confirmed this, to your interpretation, to be other than hallucination. Death's sting, grave's victory contradicted, you marched on knowing triumph was guaranteed eventually, whenever. Imagine this, then you will understand why this motley band of social outcasts were so proud. This remnant of Israel, as we also considered ourselves, regarded ourselves as kings and queens, princes and princesses, in spite of the absence of corresponding wealth, which wealth would come in time. A Rastaman referred to his wife as his queen and she to him as her king man.

Like in any situation involving people, especially in large numbers, there were animosities and enmities, but the instilled principle of one for all, all for one did work. If an Israelite observed one even with whom he was vexed, in need or trouble, he was duty bound to give a helping hand. With the application of this principle, His Majesty had said, there could be no failure. The hymn 'The tie that binds' was very significant to us, and often was sung on the Hill and at other meetings.

In this Twelve Tribes branch of Rasta, colour discrimination was practised only by the over-zealous black militants. Shem, Ham and Japheth were all represented, and every possible shade of colour in between was present, with the black skin obviously predominant. As I said, there were a few who did not accept the non-racial position, just like there were some who did not accept the Bible's authority. A few too, did not accept the prophet's leadership, just like some were not into any Jesus Christ. These dissidents were very few, added their controversy as an ingredient in the pot, and would have come into the house from one of the earlier fundamentalist Rastafarian movements. All told, for a group of such diverse socioeconomic, educational and racial backgrounds, we got on just fine, for all practical purposes. You must remember some of the brethren lived in the deep woods away from any societal influence, spurning even the wearing of shoes. Some were from a much higher social background and orientation than myself. In between, lay all types, with the pendulum skewed to what we then referred to as the 'roots'. And you had to be careful of how you related to each person, for fear of offending a group. I remember Ringo, in his enthusiasm, heeding a call for help re clothing, filling his car with some of his fancy clothes ... used. He had to beat a hasty retreat. Not even the least of them would wear used clothing.

Not to offend sensitivities or sensibilities, people like us, especially in the earlies, had to tread through the house as carefully as through a mine field. Some though, of different ilk, were pretty easy to deal with. 'Nifty Nafty' of my tribe, a partial paraplegic, was my friend, and I would sit with him in his shack or my study and reason Scripture, Israel, His Majesty, life. I learnt many things from that humble man. 'Stone Dread', on the other hand, never seemed to like me and my type, and was always throwing a negative vibe at me when he wasn't begging me something. It was common knowledge, though, that some types would try to discourage you away, but as the prophet often said, it was your responsibility to hold on to your seat. In some ways, he was a most philosophical man.

There were some within who, though not seated elders, enjoyed a form of seniority befitting the respected elite. They had been in the organ long, knew and related well with everyone, had a reasonable economic base, had helped visibly in the growth of the organ and knew how to enjoy, rightly, their status. Some were sportsmen of past glories who had spurned Babylon for the truth and this way of life. Like most Israelites, they were nice, kind hearted people, if you braved it through their countenance enough to know their spirit.

I was thinking of tying up a lease on a large old house to accommodate 'Nifty Nafty' and his crew. Ringo had helped me into the company of the said respected elite, and I had mentioned what I proposed to do. They had discouraged that, saying any expenditure like that would be better placed towards hiring a plane to take us home. Now I know that the lease of the place would have been more trouble for me. They simply would not be financially responsible enough to meet the monthly arrangement. Perfect as they were at doing His Majesty's work, in matters financial, personal they were most unreliable and irresponsible, especially if the obligation was to a Babylonian.

On the other hand, even if a plane were found, free of cost, that band of elite would not, I am now sure, leave their comfort zone for any uncivilised anywhere. Not that they weren't genuinely devoted Rasta, but they were also practical, fun-loving people.

I can now see 'Mally-Dread' on the Hill, his turn to be flown home, squirming in front of the prophet, proffering all kinds of lame excuses why he could not leave now – the same 'Mally-Dread' who was heretofore so anxious, verbally, to fly out of Babylon, homebound to mother Africa, Ethiopia in particular.

'Mouth mek fi seh anything ... talk is cheap.' Do I now know that!

A more music-loving, musically talented set of people I have never seen. The reference to singers and players of music, in the Bible, could well fit them. A very significant proportion of the membership sang well enough and/or played an instrument quite competently. Were it not that the prophet, at the time, restricted, where possible, commercial exposure of the music, as a body they would have been internationally recognised, in this regard. Not all, naturally, would touch the peak that brethren Bob from the tribe of Joseph had, but they would have done well. Was the prophet right in this decision?

132

There was, indeed, a great militancy in the approach of the brothers, as also the sisters, and I imagine that, given the existing love, unity and commitment plus godly faith, they could also give a good account in protecting themselves physically. However, in what I refer to as my second stint in the house, we held a grand celebration at a theatre in a roughish area. The proceeds of the gate had to be hurried away to a safer point. A few of the more awe-inspiring brethren would travel in the front car. Others, with me as chauffeur, would follow behind, and a sister, with more brethren, would complete the posse. One of my passengers kept saying to me annoyingly, 'Follow that car', having like myself heard these words in a movie. Following that car in my Citroën van was not easy, as it was going ridiculously fast. I worried for the sister behind, but kept following the car with the money. We eventually reached a home, parked and waited for the poor sister who finally turned up. As it turned out, the pilot car had led us into the wrong house, a stranger's house. The sister was then detailed to go back to the point of origin to get the right address. By the time she had left on her mission, the leader remembered the right address and departed top speed with the Citroën trying to keep pace. I sighed a sigh of concern for the sister's return, not having a clue as to where we had gone. Militant?

This was a freak, really, for indeed they usually did things well.

Our sisters were treated almost always with the courtesy and respect befitting women, mothers, queens at the time, though like everywhere else, absolute equality did not exist. They had their roles; and, in my view, if their views, opinion and general involvement had been more integrated into the whole operation much more would have been achieved; but then again, the entire world system is skewed against them to its detriment. Of course, they have many shortcomings, but men probably have more. Still, to every male executive group there was the female one standing behind ... behind.

Within the house, once they had borne a child, the principal responsibility of bringing it up was theirs. And did the brethren impregnate their queens prolifically! Of a truth though, the fathers were usually quite close to their offspring. In many situations, too, the virtuous woman, the queen, had the income-producing role whilst her kingman sat with the elders, so to speak, doing Jah's work. The sisters on the whole, few excepted, were wonderful, committed, helpful persons, queens indeed, as most women are. Many had taken a big social step down to be with the man they loved, to suffer with him, sacrificially, denying themselves of accustomed comfort, struggling onward, faithfully and courageously in the service of Jesus the Christ now revealed in His kingly character, His Imperial Majesty, King of Kings and Lord of Lords, Conquering Lion of the Tribe of Judah, Haile Selassie, the First. And in some cases, as in mine, the kingman was too preoccupied to remember gratitude and reciprocation.

The organ did humble many of us, thus levelling the playing field, tearing down some walls, socio-economic and otherwise. The resulting metamorphosis was interesting, to say the least, and manifested, among other ways, significantly in male-female match-ups, that the existing status quo would loathe, as certainly some parents did. Some brethren of past 'upper class' ilk took unto themselves 'brides' of origin similar to those from whence their domestic helpers had come, just as the daughters of gentry had teamed up with the sons of the ghetto.

Sisters of all races and colours were giving themselves in

'marriage' to brothers of different colours, and barriers of race as well as colour and class. Those barriers, as much as was possible, were almost automatically slid out of the way and replaced by love, unity and goodwill.

The organ was building a little house on the Hill, with a contribution made by my wife. The head contractor amongst us procured the lumber and left it at the foot of the Hill. It was meeting day. Each man, woman or child was to carry up one piece, comfortably manageable; before the meeting started each piece was settled in the appropriate place. By the next day all men of that profession were to turn up to erect the structure. By evening the next day, the shelter and basic school for the children were functional. Led by the prophet, these people could floor any with their grass roots logic.

Within the house lay skill in almost every possible area; only one doctor, one aeroplane pilot, but many in many other areas – this over two decades ago when I was actively there.

In my time, brethren and sisters from the various branches globally, usually from England and America, were always passing through, so glad to reason with us brethren from headquarters, and they were always so full of praise and so worshipful of the founder, the prophet. Brother Naphtali should rightly have received a share, albeit smaller, of the glory. Characteristically common to all those visitors I met, except one, were humility and genuine love and goodwill. The visiting brethren would time their visits to coincide with our monthly meeting, thereby undergoing, first hand, the experience of the meeting on the Hill. They were expected to address the congregation, usually carrying greetings from their neck of the woods. Their every word was applauded in true brotherly love, friendship and harmony.

Whenever we, from the original base, travelled abroad, if

there was a branch located there, attended their meetings bearing greetings from home base. And if the visit did not coincide with a meeting of theirs, we would visit their headquarters to meet and strengthen whichever brethren were present. I didn't travel abroad during my sojourn in the house.

My brethren and sisters were perfect by no stretch of imagination. They came closest to epitomising, practically, peace and love, truth and right, within my limited experience of life, but as I said they were not perfect. Our cricket coach, a most devoted and dedicated one, a member of the executive, a Simeonite of the second set of executives (second as opposed to first or third rank), was a good man. We arranged a cricket competition with us competing individually as opposed to in teams. The coach participated as a competitor. I was on good form and on my way to winning the competition, with the coach in second place. Starky Dread was the officiating umpire and, I know, gave me out when I clearly wasn't even remotely out. I appealed to the coach, but unearthed no sympathy, as he went on to win. It was good for morale that the coach won, but I was disappointed that he had not stood up for honesty. I would have.

I remember visiting my young beautiful platonic girlfriend, when soon, thereafter, a fairly well fed first executive came by. I didn't accept it then but he was interested in 'checking' her. He sought of her food for himself and the brethren he came with. She had none to offer at such short notice. He chided her for her inability to provide him food, and kept on gibing her about it. Now this poor little girl had such difficulty paying her rent and sustaining herself at teacher training college, I knew not how she managed, much less to be expected to feed these brethren. I was disappointed, but seethed only inwardly. Little did I know that people, even the best of them, are not always thoughtful and compassionate.

Of a truth, the house was full of much peace and love and goodness, but there were conflicts often, and quite a few reached the hill for resolution and punishment. Many, too, for one reason or another, never came up for public scrutiny. Oppression can make even a wise man mad, so the Proverbs tell me. Imagine, therefore the numerous turmoils and conflicts experienced before the state of insanity clutched you. Given the level of financial paucity within the house, and the constant oppression from the system and society, it was commendable that the conflicts were so relatively few. As I said before, the brethren and sisters were not perfect.

There were some real women stalwarts in the organisation, women who could be counted on to do whatever needed to be done, and excellently; women who were prepared, despite their lesser status, to chastise the brethren verbally, whilst lifting and encouraging them to greater heights. And where most of us were 'yes men' to the prophet, some women were more prepared to express a contrary viewpoint, albeit gently and inoffensively. There were really some lion-hearted women within the house.

Other than Colin Lamb, there were quite a few outstanding men too. The Asher executive, the unofficial treasurer, was one such. He provided help in almost every area, and, whilst running his business, found time to be there for the organisation and the membership, to excellent proportions, during my time therein.

Rain or shine, near or far, a member very seldom missed a meeting, and the behaviour of us considered outcasts, hooligans was so exemplary in many regards that the leader must have been worthy of commendation. The executives, though, should have had more of a say in the administration, and a better line of command should have been established and succession planned for. No man is an island. Did not even Moses accept administrative counsel of Jethro, his father-in-law an outsider, even?

Jehovah's Witnesses study their Scriptures diligently, as do many other denominations, but none devours it as passionately as a Twelve Tribes Rasta, it seemed to me. There is a tendency though, of most religious groups to a skewed interpretation consistent with that groups beliefs.

9

The End

What is to be must be, so what was to be had to be. I lost some money as a result of this Rasta involvement, but I gained a spirituality that before was missing from my life. Who is to tell; stupid introverted me might even make it to Heaven.

I spent less than four years actually involved in the movement, and that phase began almost twenty years ago. Still, since that time I have kept in touch from a distance with happenings within the house. In spite of the time since my active involvement, it all seems like yesterday's happenings, and in spite of an occasional tendency to think that I wasted quality and quantity time, that period seems to have been the most significant of my life. To tell you the truth the Twelve Tribes of Israel seems to have claimed a special piece of my heart, almost irretrievably. I keep wondering why it was so important for me to be outstanding. Why couldn't I, like others, settle for a low-keyed existence within?

During my time, it was really a heavy, heavy movement. Once you were in, you felt that there could be no reason to go back to whatever you had left behind. In fact, you assumed your tribe name and the membership related to you thus:

Ringo Judah or Naphti Brods. You just felt that you had found the only worthwhile spot in creation. And the miraculous events I experienced during those years confirmed that, for me, that was where it was at. I prayed for cash, and, within minutes, where there was none, some materialised. I prayed for rain and the sun receded to allow a downpour. I had paralysing growth pains and I merely prayed them away. That's how close I felt to God in those days.

My wife and child were, naturally, my closest kin and the love I had for my daughter was as much as a father can have for a child. I was that day studying and pondering on the book of Job in the Holy Bible. I read of his suffering and felt his deep pain, to the extent that was possible. Could I, I asked myself, bear similar burdens and still love God? That night, when I arrived home my house seemed empty and a sense of foreboding overwhelmed me. Something felt awfully wrong. The helper told me my wife and child were upstairs sleeping. Strangely enough, the door was locked from the inside. Knock and shout as I did, there was no response. Momentarily the thought arose that they were dead. My first response was to wail like a bereaved mother. My second was to cast my thoughts in the direction of the Almighty. Then I remembered Job, and found righteousness enough to say 'God giveth and God taketh away, blest be God the Almighty'. Needless to say, they were very much alive but God had run a mock event on me and found me reasonably prepared.

An area in which most of us had failed was in worshipping the prophet almost to the same extent as we did God. Now I look back and see that most of us, a few women exempted, agreed with him even when he was talking foolishness, often on subjects he knew nothing about. And those of us with more expert knowledge allowed him to ramble on, accepting what he said as law. And if for example, he said something grammatically incorrect, or mispronounced a word, from thenceforth was his style copied, as opposed to that which was the right way.

Many of us refused to use our education, training and experience to work out solutions to even our minor problems, seeking consultation with him on everything. I, for one, ascribed to him more respectful fatherhood than I had, at any time, afforded my earthly father.

I devoted some very important years of my life to this movement/cause at a very crucial stage of my life, and claim the right to express, fearlessly, my opinions and findings in respect of this matter, as in respect to any other. Some may think otherwise, but that is their concern. I try always to speak the truth, certainly as I perceive it, which of course means I could be wrong, although perhaps not often.

Early in 1997 I attended a Twelve Tribes dance and stage show at the students' union on the university campus. As usual, I had a largish amount of money with which to spread joy amongst these persons I had not seen for a long time, whilst enjoying the music and its nostalgic reminders of that most significant era of my life. I digress to say again I love Twelve Tribes and will feel a 'little thing' in my heart for them for ever, though I parted company with them many years ago. I have always kept track, interestedly, over those years, through members I am in touch with, and by attending some of their functions, open to the public like the one referred to earlier, to which story I will soon return. I will also tell you later how and why I left the organisation, but first let me quickly tell you what I gained from those significant years within that cult, which forms a part of why they are likely, always, to claim a part of my heart.

I currently have a passionate love for the study of the Bible and the corresponding reading habit. I have a love for God that cannot die, and a desire to serve and please Him. The Bible knowledge and the love of God no man can deprive me of. These I gained from my involvement in the Twelve Tribes of Israel. My current understanding of people from all walks of life and my proclivity to ongoing benevolence, habits I have happily indoctrinated my children into, were also byproducts of my association with the Twelve Tribes. Numerous other important things I learnt there will assist me greatly, if in fact I decide to embark on my own ministry. Twelve Tribes was more than an ordinary institution of learning for me, and I thank the good Lord for purifying me by smelting me therein, drawing me through those scorching coals. Many thanks are also in order for the prophet, the elders and the membership; but that's all I owe them, for I did give my all to do my part.

The function in question was open to the public and advertised as such, so, along with my nephew, I paid the entry. From the moment I entered I felt bad vibes: members who months ago I ate and drank and chatted amiably with were going on as if they had never met me in life. Persons, even, who had recently sought my assistance, treated me like the devil himself. They all passed me and looked away with scorn; one found it difficult to ignore me and whispered his 'Hi' as he passed by. I decided against leaving. Theirs was the right to do as they pleased, mine, a paying patron, was to stay if I wished. I was terribly disappointed in them, though, when my purchases were rudely served and my unfinished drinks removed. Common decency, I told my nephew, is a feature they used to abound in. Was their instruction from the prophet or did it originate from Levi who was in charge of that bar? Recently, I had seen much of Levi, and as is my nature I hailed him enthusiastically. His response was less than lukewarm and even less so the next three times. I then decided that Levi could kiss my ass, for indeed my greeting him was born of nothing else but good upbringing, and a cordial, amicable personality. I still decided to hang around a bit more until the end of the stage show, but when the prophet muscled into the stage show rendering his version of some songs, I concluded that they had forgotten that many of us present, having paid our way, spending valuable time and money, had come to be entertained.

On departing, I took a last look at them: grown men, many older than me, incapable of making their own decisions as to whom to talk to. They fell even further in my estimation. I drove away concluding that that was my final severing of ties.

In 1978, the herb and everything else had taken its toll and I ended up in hospital. Later, I was diagnosed as being manic depressive, and hospitalisation was as a result of a massive manic episode. For months I was in the hospital, and to date, I can't remember a member of the organisation except, of course, my wife and my sister, coming to visit me; me, who was always there for anyone and everyone.

Within the house there had been times when I wondered if I was in fact on the right road. This thought usually came when I wasn't high. By the time I had taken the next draw, I regretted and repented of the earlier thought. Those months in the hospital, without ingestion of the herb, cured me of the habit. Back to sanity, my mind was filled with those earlier thoughts. The insanity indeed was a Godsend. I cleaned myself off and sought and gained employment again as a real estate salesman. My wife and myself, now inseparably close again, investigated our religious options. Knowing what we thought we knew, we could not be satisfied by the established churches. The religious principle of the Twelve Tribes of Israel we believed in, so we decided on a continuation, which I referred to in an earlier chapter as the second stint. Of course, she made it quite clear, and I understood, the herb was not to be interfered with by me.

Working in Babylon and functioning as an active member was very difficult, but I kept on doing my best in both spheres. Anyhow, to shorten the story, the house decided to purchase premises for their headquarters and approached me, visiting my place of employment in great numbers. Eventually I found them the ideal property, a prime one. The purchase ran into all sorts of problems, all of which I maneuvered skilfully around, sacrificing my commission interest and that of my bosses. At one stage, to avert a crisis, my wife and I withdrew seven thousand of the eight thousand dollars we had saved, in order to ensure the procurement of the relevant titles. A part of the deposit, sent in cash by the prophet, was said by the secretary to contain some bad notes. She was adamant that the bad notes were part of that sent; equally so was the prophet that these did not originate from him. In the interest of peace I offered to bear the loss. I can hardly remember, in my entire career, a transaction that gave me so much trouble and worry, and cost me instead of compensating me. Incidentally, the company did reimburse me that seven thousand dollars.

Eventually, I was able to deliver to the prophet the two titles for the premises adjoining each other, which I had already procured possession of for the house. There remained but one comparatively small matter left to be solved, namely the removal of a caveat from the titles, and I worked assiduously at completing this, spending my own money to purchase legal assistance.

Israel had possession and the two titles free and clear except for the existing caveat, yet I could hear mumblings concerning how I had handled the matter. I realised what was happening; they wanted someone to crucify and I, with one foot in, one foot out seemed a likely candidate. At any meeting, all the prophet had to do was imply ineffectiveness or betrayal on my part, and the membership, every man and woman, except my wife and sister, would turn their scorn on me, especially now that part of me had a foot in Babylon. I made my decision. They would crucify me behind my back as I would attend no meetings until the caveat was removed.

During this time, I got some time to think. Levi and myself had been assigned the task of seeing to the matter of the purchase. Levi was of little help. I could truthfully say that, single handedly, I had swung for them their most major step, despite all sorts of hurdles in the way. They now owned a most centrally located HQ with accommodation facilities for some. The price negotiated was way below market price, and I had pumped back my commission and got the company to do likewise, even picking up further losses re the bad notes, in order to ease their financial requirement. I had also risked my meagre savings to save the transaction. The holding was a prime one that would escalate in value extremely rapidly and had various options for usage, commercial or residential; it was a prime property indeed, with two separate titles, with two road frontages. I had done wonderfully well for Israel, certainly in this regard. Yet never did I hear anyone say thanks; instead they seemed waiting to lynch me.

It was then that I started to look at Israel with more objectively critical eyes. The caveat matter was going to be someone else's chore to deal with; I had simply done more than my share. And these people, so contentious, so suspicious, so unreasonable, so prepared to condemn without making any effort to ascertain the truth of a matter – could they, in fact, be God's people?

At that time, I had embarked on my own real estate business and was doing reasonably well. At that time older brethren of the house, not elders, were allowed to promote one dance monthly. Eight of the twelve, on the suggestion of the prophet, they said, approached me for loan capital. I granted a loan to each, and all but one repaid me. Twenty-one other brethren approached me for smaller more personal loans. Two repaid me partially, nineteen I saw again only if I ran into them. I wondered again how chosen could the likes of those be. And if I did pass through the HQ, everyone wanted something from me; it was like a den of beggars. Frankly, though, it had always been like this, except that I was only now prepared to accept the reality and truth: from before conversion to now, a feeding tree is what I represented most to many brethren. Still, to be fair there were many upright brothers and sisters whose behaviour was above reproach in all regards.

The Twelve Tribes of Israel had earlier enveloped my life and being, and this was not something you forget. A part of me was still attached to them emotionally, and although there was little direct involvement in their activities I kept an ear out for what was happening in the organ. In the 1980s quite a few of the foundation stalwarts were kicked out. Apparently they had an opposing view to the prophet on one issue or another, and of course if you expressed a view, however good, that was contrary to that of the prophet, the membership backed him as he kicked you out. In this regard, we had been all like yes men, and as a result, on many occasions justice was not well dispensed. In fact we had all worshipped the prophet too much. These were not the olden days; other people had good ideas and inspiration too!

Often in these 1980s, sitting in my study or lying in my bed, I reminisced on that period of my life. I must have been a mad man, a brave man or a God fearing man to give up the comforts I had worked so hard for to become a Twelve Tribe Rasta. In retrospect, I saw where I had ascribed to all and sundry, including the prophet, too much respect and credibility. I dwarfed myself too much in unearned obeisance to them all. The prophet, I chuckled to myself, was so cunning, he managed to maintain normal hair length whilst leading a body of predominantly dreads. He was a real shrewd operator. I thought back on the major objective of the organ and the weepy cries of the brothers to go back home. Yet if the truth be told, at best, most wanted to visit and then return to Jamaica.

I did learn a lot within the organisation, and although I would have been a very wealthy man if I hadn't heeded that call, I don't really regret the experience. My religious organisation, though primarily Christian, will adapt some of the good principles I learnt therein.

Will Israel survive? I wondered. Has the prophet attended to the matter of succession, or is he too busy enjoying the power? Twelve Tribes of Israel was the pride of some poor and downtrodden people, plus others. Why is it deteriorating so? I remember how much care was put into dispelling the misconceptions the public had of us. They saw us, for example, as untidy and unclean. As a result, when we rented a place to have a function, we returned it spotlessly clean.

God is not a distant concept but a lived reality. This is how I see it and have reproduced it in literary works. I must confess that this, too, I picked up from within the Twelve Tribes. Yet they were so contentious, I now remember; you had to be so careful of what you did or said. Still there was good in this in that there was a conscious effort on one's part to do that which was right at all times.

As I lay in my bed, the Twelve Tribes on my mind, I felt it to my heart for certain elders who had so sacrificed for the organ and were so unceremonially pushed out, unjustly it seemed to me. I escaped the nostalgic stranglehold of the Twelve Tribes on my mind, on the note that, born on 24 January, I could really have been a Joseph instead of a Naphtali.

Ever since severing significant ties with the Twelve Tribes I have been searching for the real truth concerning His Majesty. After all, I had served him most obediently as the Almighty God. I still now in 1997 have all the pictures and literature pertaining to him, and have continued to study the Scriptures more or less daily. The Scriptures tell most plainly that the key figure and route to God is Jesus Christ. I see this clearly in my study of the following topics, among others: salvation recognising the spirit of God, eternal life, overcoming the world, judgement, every knee shall bow, the way of the truth and the life, dominion over death. There is absolutely no controversy, Jesus is the route given to man to overcome this evil world.

His Majesty, to me, is a most important personage, the most important I have or will see in my lifetime. A most righteous and God fearing being, who, by virtue of ascendancy to the

throne God Almighty relates to, was indeed King of Kings
and Lord of Lords, with a lineage traceable back to King
Solomon and by extension King David to whom God made
that covenant, referred to as the Davidic covenant. If related
by genealogy to King David, His Majesty therefore was
related genealogically to the marvellous Jesus, the Christ.
History shows that from time to time God sends one with a
spirit that reawakens others to goodness and righteousness.
His Majesty was such a one, and my reading of his history
proves to me that he was a very good and righteous man. In
his writings on Jesus Christ he ascribes to him the greatest
praise and the only route to 'life in its fullest sense'.

I will always remember His Majesty with love, as the route
through which I passed on my way to a life in Jesus Christ.

Many Rastas, I now realise, are factoring Jesus Christ more
significantly and meaningfully into their doctrine. That, I
think, is very good; for 'who is he that overcometh the world,
but he that believeth that Jesus Christ is the son of God' (i
John 5:5). Some however, are hurriedly discarding His Majesty.
My advice is respect him and put him in the proper perspective.

Twelve Tribes was a learning experience for many of us. I
can't speak for others, but for myself, I feel like a graduate
who must use that knowledge, plus that from other sources,
to influence my life, and that of others, positively to good, in
the hope of eternal blissful life. Those whose calling it is to
remain in the Twelve Tribes must so remain and, guided by a
good conscience, do what is theirs to do.

In closing let me just say of my experience within the
Twelve Tribes of Israel, 'It was a bitter sweet mix of good and
bad'.

Postscript

Yes, I am still alive, thank God, and kicking, and have matured enough to be now able to laugh at myself, and others too. I can laugh at many things also, past and present, and now possess clarity of mind sufficient to see into the future. I am now my own seer. I still feel like a child of God, a chosen, an Israelite, even, for I know from the New Testament that a Jew is one inwardly.

I no longer smoke the herb and haven't for years, but I do remember how it made me feel then. The pleasant aspects of it had, among other experiences, given me the feeling that I had unearthed a great secret of life – one peculiar to the chosen few, one the majority were ignorant of and not worthy of partaking of.

In my further reminiscences, I can't but remember how on the day His Imperial Majesty was announced as dead I felt as if his spirit had come into my heart; I felt His presence in my being more than ever before and I loved Him even more. I remember, most vividly, the mental turmoil and my personal deliberations when the Twelve Tribes seemed to my conscience and my intellect the right spiritual road to travel. But my conscious self resisted stoutly until the Book of Jonah cornered me, pointing out the futility, punishment, even, of trying to run away from the calling of God.

When I had eventually pulled away from the organisation, though not formally and absolutely finally, and had set up my business, the brethren invaded me in droves, with all kinds of stories, seeking financial assistance. Less than one in ten even attempted repayment. Whether they now saw me as Babylon or they were always this bad in respect of repayments I don't know. I do know though that the prophet, possessing faults, too, had always encouraged repayment of debts and all but one he had directed to me, at that time, did make good his reimbursement.

Among the benefits gained from my experience within the organisation was the ability to know what to expect, to an extent, characteristically, from a person by the month in which he or she was born. I truly learnt many other things too, important things which will be of assistance to my pursuits present and future.

I know so much more about people from all walks of life. This elder's wife had given birth to her first child in the comfort and peace of my home, being a friend of my wife. As soon as we started to pull back from active involvement in the movement, she was one of the first to throw stones. She claimed she had never been friends of ours and had merely used our facilities for convenience. In recent times, I have often seen her husband and hailed him, but his response has always seemed so deliberately hesitant that I have ceased acknowledging him; in fact, my intention was not to beg friendship but instead to be cordial, courteous and polite.

In some ways, I must confess, based on my behaviour within the house, if you had to name something after the world's biggest fool then it would have to bear my name. I must have been mad long before I was hospitalised, probably from the time I started smoking the herb. It's a good thing I can now laugh at myself.

I had written the lyrics for and produced the recording of a musical disc entitled *Thanksgiving Song*, a song of praise to God. Bloody Dread, a Twelve Tribe brethren, had written and arranged a best-selling song, and was in touch with the current music trends. In my stints in the house, 'Bloody' and I had got on quite well so I searched him out to assist me in improving my little song of thanks to God. I was going to the country so he decided to tour with me. He entered the car, spliff in hand. On the way he built and lit another. This type of anti-law behaviour I had long escaped, being now again a respectable real estate broker. I hinted at the discomfort, but didn't quite insist firmly that Bloody put out the spliff, as I should have, since he had entered my car. As I walked the lands for sale with the owner, Bloody rolled and lit another. Didn't he realise his conduct was inappropriate? As we embarked to leave, he lit another, as I headed out to pass by my sister's home, nearby, at the district where I was born and grown. In my sister's home I could smell the unmistakable scent of ganja as Bloody was at it again. Was I ever like that, I wondered, so addicted and unmindful of sensitivities and sensibilities? Now, the police of the parish were on an anti-ganja drive and a reign of terror existed in this and adjoining districts. Bloody, his locks flowing, at the gate, had attracted the attention of some of the local dreads, and much to the disgust of my sister, a few spliffs were being enjoyed. As it turned out, Bloody wanted a taste of the local stuff and one of the dreads went to his home to fetch some. Later, we saw him returning with two policemen with very large guns behind him, marching him humiliatingly on the road to the lock-up, six miles away. I felt so much rage against Bloody for getting the fellow in all this trouble. He too seemed very hurt by what he had caused. Heading back to Kingston, he did not cease the herb smoking, but it was considerably reduced. Before leaving for town, I sought out a friend, an old schoolmate, a man of great contacts in the parish. I gave him some money and asked him to solve the plight of the arrested man as best he could. All the way over to town I felt like a dog for having carried this Bloody anywhere, and even musically he had not come up with any real suggestions. Next day, my friend told me that the fellow had been released and I felt so relieved.

Bloody enjoyed his last trip with me. I was tolerant of his bad habits for I, too, had passed that way, Rasta, but was I that bad and annoying to others?

How the poor live is usually no business of the other classes, but it should be. Better understanding would lesson tensions that can erupt. I give just a little example. Early in my first stint within the house, a brethren told me he was going to check me to discuss a matter, at a particular time on a particular day. At the appointed time, he did not show up; I waited an hour and then left. The next time I saw him I could sense his anger towards me. After discussion I realised what had happened. He lived far from my home in the violent ghetto, had braved bullets and taken two different buses to reach my home. He had no more money for the fare back, and knew that I would have provided him with it, instead, with nobody at my home, he had to walk all the way back, through all sorts of terrible areas. It dawned on me that my impatience could have caused my brethren bodily harm if not death.

The Twelve Tribe experience was a most significant one to

me and I reminisce on it quite often, even now. How ironic it seemed to me that the older ones in Babylon always directed us to the reading of the Bible and rejoiced when a child showed passion for the Scriptures. Once in, or contemplating conversion to the Twelve Tribes and passionately studying the Scriptures, the same people complained of too much time and seriousness being applied to the Bible, the same one the reading of which they had encouraged heretofore.

I can't also forget the shock and the astonishment when I stopped long enough and pulled away sufficiently far to look at the system existing then. The injustice, the prejudices, the corruption, the wholesale nastiness – I knew, even then, nothing founded on such could prosper.

In some ways, now looking from afar, the Twelve Tribes is not a bunch of innocents either. As I sit in my study and do my writings, religious ones especially, I can't but marvel what a clear understanding and concept I now have of God and related matters, enough even to share to the enlightenment of others. Twenty-one years ago, I had not a clue in this regard – no concept, no understanding, nothing besides unanswered questions – a state I now know most people, even those close to me, are now in,   ignorance. For this reason, I wish to share my knowledge and experiences. Sometimes though, I don't feel too kindly inclined to people generally, because my experiences have taught me how suspect they can be. I don't know that they or the system they uphold have, in fact, changed significantly since the time of Christ.